# LINDA SKEENS
## Blue Ribbon Kitchen

# LINDA SKEENS
## Blue Ribbon Kitchen

RECIPES & TIPS FROM AMERICA'S FAVORITE COUNTY FAIR CHAMPION

83 press

83 Press
2323 2nd Avenue North
Birmingham, AL 35203
83Press.com

ISBN 978-0-9835984-7-3
Printed in China

83
press

# Foreword

## by Mason Moussette

THE HEADLINES FROM JUNE 27TH, 2022, read as follows: "New 'World's Ugliest Dog' Named," "Ben Affleck's 10-Year-Old Son Backed a Lambo into a BMW," and "Internet Trying to Find Woman Who Dominated County Fair's Baking Contest."

It was the third headline that caught my attention.

Linda Skeens had won Best Cake, Best Pie, Best Brownies, Best Jelly, Best Jam, Best Applesauce, Best Apple Butter, Best Pumpkin Butter, Best Sauerkraut, and Best Spaghetti Sauce at the Virginia-Kentucky District Fair.

If that wasn't enough, her strawberry fudge won Best Overall Baked Good. She also placed first, second, AND third in three baking categories: Best Cookies, Best Bread, and Best Candy. And for good measure, she swept all three embroidery categories and placed for her crafts, too. Even with too many wins to list, no one publicly stepped forward to claim the glory. The internet went into a flurry, asking "Who is Linda Skeens?" The question was practically shouted from every corner of the world.

She became an internet legend overnight, with Jordan Keyes creating "The Ballad of Linda Skeens" and people like Josh Clark commenting, "Chuck Norris beats everyone except Linda Skeens." People wanted to know who this Linda Skeens was! Was she a recent empty nester or a divorcée who had free time on her hands and a passion for baking and crafting? Was she the 90-year-old grandmother whose one joy in life was to cook for her family? Did she buy off the judges? Was she the only one who entered? Was she even real? The world needed to know.

As a morning radio host, I had a quirky story segment that aired during the 6 a.m. hour that Linda's story would be perfect for, but I didn't realize my audience would respond so passionately when I went to social media with a fact-finding battle cry: "Are YOU Linda Skeens? Do you KNOW Linda Skeens? We must find Linda Skeens!"

The internet is a wild and wonderful place, and soon after I posted about Linda, my TikTok video (posted on @masononthemic), went viral. I had main stream reporters reaching out to me to see if I had found her yet. I had not. And to be honest, I had not really been looking. I talked about it on my radio show, posted about it on social media, and then I went home

to watch reality TV. But the response made me stop and think: if I can find information about my Bumble dates knowing only their first name, alma mater, and niece's age, I could surely find THE Linda Skeens! And so, I did.

In a short time, I did what no one else was able to. I knew her first and last name. I knew she lived in Virginia, and I had been tagged in potential relatives' posts. Turning to an internet background site, I gave them $9.99, and they gave me a list of possible Lindas. She was the second person I called.

"Is this the Linda Skeens that swept the Virginia-Kentucky District Fair?" I asked. "Yes, it is." "Linda, my name is Mason, and I'm a morning radio host; would you have time for a quick interview?" "Yes." I couldn't believe she agreed so quickly. I rushed back to the studio, and the rest, as they say, is history.

I quickly found out that Linda was not really any of the things the internet imagined. Instead, she was a sweet and creative 74-year-old grandmother who enjoys cooking for her family and entering local fairs. And she loves a good competition!

While the internet was shocked by her sweeping the fair competition, this was certainly not her first rodeo in collecting blue ribbons. Having done this for over thirty years, she was not prepared for the media frenzy that arose one afternoon in June. Linda was completely taken aback with the attention in the most genuinely humble and gracious way. I knew that as soon as I posted that I had found THE Linda Skeens that her life was going to change big time. Huge opportunities were coming her way, and it wasn't long before she called to tell me she signed a deal for her dream cookbook.

I've been able to chat with her a few times now, and I continue to be blown away by her humility and kindness. She's sincerely happy to be here, teaching people about something she loves, and it shows in this cookbook. I was lucky enough to have her send me some of the recipes she shares here, and wow! All the hype was worth it. She didn't win those ribbons for nothing, and I'm excited to now replicate those treats for my own friends and family. And, if you see me winning every category at my county fair one day, will you pretend not to know I'm just using Linda's recipes? If so, I'll do the same for you.

# Contents

Foreword.................................................5

Introduction...........................................8

CHAPTER 1: Canning............................. 14

CHAPTER 2: Dips & Spreads................... 40

CHAPTER 3: Appetizers & Snacks ........56

CHAPTER 4: Soups & Salads................. 78

CHAPTER 5: Main Dishes..................... 100

CHAPTER 6: Casseroles ...................... 130

CHAPTER 7: Sides................................ 148

CHAPTER 8: Breads............................. 168

CHAPTER 9: Cakes ............................... 190

CHAPTER 10: Cookies & Pies ............... 216

CHAPTER 11: Fudges & Treats ............. 232

Recipe Index........................................ 254

A Final Note of Thanks....................... 255

# Introduction

**FOR MOST OF THE INTERNET,** my story begins on June 13, 2022, when the Virginia-Kentucky District Fair posted the winners for their Home Economic Exhibits. I won dozens of ribbons, including seven Best Overall for my baked goods, canning, and crafts. I'm not on social media, so I didn't see that post. I found out when I went to collect my goods at the end of the fair. I hoped to pick up a few ribbons, but I walked away with a lot more. I learned I had gone "viral."

Soon, my name was everywhere I turned. They were talking about me on the news, and my kids and grandkids kept sharing posts and videos of people talking about me. Still, I didn't reach out to anyone. I thought it would blow over. After all, this is what I do every year. I enter the fairs. I win a few ribbons, and then I go home to start prepping for next year's fairs.

Except, that didn't go exactly as I imagined. The news stations struggled to find me, but one radio DJ in Dallas, Texas, did. Mason Moussette (Mason on the Mic) called me one afternoon on my home phone, and I did my first interview that day. I thought that would be the end of it, but people became even more interested after that call. I visited tv shows and did radio interviews, even one based out of Europe!

I thought flying on my first airplane and going on the *Today Show* would be the biggest highlight from last year; then one afternoon in August, I got a call from Hoffman Media in Birmingham, Alabama. Not only did they want to put me in a magazine

*Visiting* Talk of Alabama *in Birmingham*

(*Taste of the South*), but also, they wanted to publish my cookbook. I spent some time talking on the phone with Anna in their book division, 83 Press, and I knew I wanted them to help me tell my story and share my recipes. I invited her to come visit, and the next week, Anna was knocking on my door with two executives from the company, Brian and Greg. As I sat around my table, laughing with the team from 83 Press, I signed my first cookbook contract. In a few short months, I went from my regular, annual county fair entry to a cookbook author. Some days, I still can't believe the gift this journey has been.

I have been incredibly blessed with a good life. I was born in Dante, a coal mining town in Virginia. At its peak in the 1930s, it was a bustling town of over 4,000 people. When I was growing up, the mines were the central focus of our town. Everyone had family who worked in or for the mines. It was just part of how life was back then. My daddy was a coal miner, and my mommy took care of us kids. I still remember how we didn't always have running water in the house back then, so Mommy would have to get pots of it to warm up on the stove for everyone to wash with. Even though we didn't have a lot, she always made sure we were cared for.

My brothers and sisters

Mommy was a good cook. People would pay her to make fudge every year, but I was not a natural like her. When Frank and I got married, I was terrible at cooking, but I learned along the way. Mommy and Celia, Frank's mom, taught me a lot, and I got better.

*Frank and me with a handmade gift from our son*

I stayed home and raised our three children, Frank Jr., Cathy, and Elizabeth. They were my joy. Eventually, they grew up, and I needed something to fill my time. With my love of cooking, it was only natural I got a job up the road at the school cooking for the kids there. I loved working with those ladies and cooking for those kids.

Now, I'm retired, and it's just Frank and me at home, but I can't seem to stop cooking. I love making food for church or for family gatherings, but I really love entering fairs. It's been forty years since I entered my first fair. I got a blue ribbon for my pillowcases back in 1983, and I was hooked. I've entered every year since. Now, I enter dozens of categories and spend the whole year prepping for the next year. Entering fairs is one of my favorite things, and I hope to keep doing it for many more years.

Fairs have been a lifeline through a few hard years. We lost our son, Frank Jr., nine years ago, which devastated our family. Just as we began to heal, COVID-19 hit and my daughter Cathy lost her husband, and we lost my brother, sister-in-law, and nephew. Being creative and cooking has allowed me an outlet during our grieving. Crafts and cooking helped me to bring joy to those I love, which has been a huge blessing.

When I was diagnosed with Leukemia in 2021, I turned to my crafts and cooking yet again. It's been a hard journey, but the doctors say I'm doing great. There's no cure, but they've said with treatment, I could live another 10 to 20 years. I'm 74 now, and I've had a good, long life. Over the last few years, I have learned to take every day as a gift that wasn't promised, and I try to celebrate every happiness that has been sent my way.

*A cute barn I made for the fair*

To my new friends and supporters: Thank you for giving me even more moments to celebrate this year. It feels real good knowing people appreciate something you love doing. This book is filled with recipes I've gathered over my lifetime that have brought me joy (and some blue ribbons). Some are family staples, and others have been passed down from friends and loved ones over the years. Cooking has always been a way for me to show love to my family and community. My food isn't fancy, but it fed my children and helped them grow into loving adults. I hope you enjoy these recipes and use them to continue feeding your families for years to come. Maybe you'll even be inspired to enter a few fairs along the way—I hope to see you there.

*Me with all my ribbons*

# Dedication

I dedicate this book to everyone who has inspired me and been there for me all these years: my husband Frank, my children, grandchildren, friends, and church family. Thank you for sharing your time, encouraging words, and recipes with me. I also dedicate this book to my new internet friends and followers: Thank you for supporting me before you even knew who I was. I appreciate all the love you've given. This book wouldn't have been possible without you. The last year has been an unexpected whirlwind, and I feel so blessed to be welcoming you into my kitchen.

## My Kitchen Prayer

God Bless my little kitchen
and all who enter in,
whether they are friends
or my next of kin.

God Bless every nook and corner
and all my pots and pans,
bless all the food I've prepared
with my loving hands.

The smell of homemade rolls
when they are starting to bake,
you just can't wait
for one of them to take.

At Christmas time I love
to make and fix every dish,
when my family isn't here
their presence I miss.

It's only a cup of coffee
or a piece of pie,
we sit around the table and chat
about all the days gone by.

So dear Lord, I ask you
Bless me and my family today,
as we hug and say good-bye
and go on our separate ways.

# A GUIDE TO MY BLUE RIBBON KITCHEN

## Appalachian Words to Know

**Hollow**—pronounced holler; a small valley where people live

**Reach Me**—hand me

**Mess**—a hearty serving

**Blinked**—the souring of milk

**Cream**—evaporated milk

**Sop**—gravy

**Aingern**—onion

**Mushmelon**—cantaloupe

**Soup beans**—brown beans, like pintos, usually served with cornbread

## Family Names to Know

**Frank**
my husband

**Delia and Henry Wright**
my parents

**Celia and Charlie Skeens**
Frank's parents

**Lilybell, Carl, Jerry, Andrew, David, and Sammy**
my siblings

**Frank Jr., Cathy, and Elizabeth**
my children

I am also blessed with 5 grandchildren and 2 great-grandchildren.

## Throughout this book you'll see

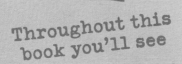

### A Blue Ribbon Symbol

A small blue ribbon at the top of some recipes marks what I've won blue ribbons for at the county fairs, so you know they'll be good!

### Original Poetry

I love being creative and writing poems when I'm inspired.

### Blue Ribbon Tips

These larger blue ribbons are full of helpful tips and ideas to try in your own kitchen.

# Scripture For a Faithful Life

*These are some of the Bible verses I remind myself of each day. They encourage me in the good times and comfort me in the hard times. My faith is important to me, and I'm thankful for a loving savior. God is always present—He holds us in His hands.*

**Psalm 46:1, KJV**

God is our refuge and strength,
a very present help in trouble.

**Proverbs 3:5, KJV**

Trust in the Lord with all thine heart.

**2 Timothy 1:7, KJV**

For God hath not given us the spirit
of fear; but of power, of love, and of
a sound mind.

**Mark 11:22-24, KJV**

And Jesus answering saith unto them, Have
faith in God. For verily I say unto you, That
whosoever shall say unto this mountain, Be
thou removed, and be thou cast into the sea;
and shall not doubt in his heart, but shall
believe that those things which he saith shall
come to pass; he shall have whatsoever he
saith. Therefore I say unto you, What things
soever ye desire, when ye pray, believe that
ye receive them, and ye shall have them.

# CHAPTER 1

# Canning

It's important to teach younger generations how to can because it's a dying art. People used to can because they had to. When I was growing up, we only had fresh fruits and vegetables in the spring, summer, and fall. We had to can them when they were in season to make it through the winter. It may not be as necessary these days, but I always like to have a variety of my canned foods at the ready. I also like to try new recipes and combinations—it keeps life interesting!

Canned items in my storage building at home

I've won a lot of ribbons for my canning

# Canning How-to

*If you've never canned before, just follow these steps and give it a try!*

1. Begin by heating the jars. Place them in a large pot on the stove and submerge them in enough water to cover. Bring the water just to a boil before turning off the heat. Keep them in the hot water until you use them. Make sure no chips are on the top of your jars. They won't seal if there are any.

2. Prepare what you are canning according to your recipe.

3. Take the jars out of the hot water with tongs and empty the jars. Fill the jars with your jam, jelly, vegetable, etc., leaving ½-inch of headspace. Using a nonmetal spatula, remove any air bubbles.

## Important Reminders

- When canning anything, use Ball or Kerr canning jars. Most fairs require one of these brands.
- The jars must be heated before use for canning to sterilize them and prevent breaking.
- Never place your glass jars directly into a pot on heat. Either use a water bath canner or place a wet kitchen towel on the bottom of a large saucepot. If you don't, your jars will shatter.

4. Wipe off the tops of each jar. Place a lid on each jar, and then screw a band on each jar.

5. Place a wet towel on the bottom of a canner or large pot (or use a metal rack). Cover with water until the water is two inches above lids. Process for the amount of time specified in the recipe.

6. Once the process is done, remove the jars from the canner with tongs and place on a wire rack or dish towel on the counter. Allow them to cool naturally at room temperature for 12 to 24 hours.

7. Test the lids to make sure they are sealed. If they are sealed, you might hear a "pop" sound. Remove the band and try to lift the lid off with your fingertips. If you cannot lift it off and the center does not flex up and down, the lid has a good seal.

# Chow Chow

*This is the way my mommy made her Chow Chow. It is very good with pinto beans and Mexican Cornbread (recipe page 183).*

*Makes about 7 pints*

1     **medium head cabbage (2-3 pounds), chopped**
5     **medium onions, chopped**
4     **green bell peppers, chopped**
4     **red bell peppers, chopped**
4     **banana peppers, seeded and chopped**
2     **green tomatoes, chopped**
¼     **cup pickling salt**
1½     **tablespoons yellow mustard**
5     **cups distilled white vinegar, divided**
2     **cups white sugar**
1     **tablespoon mustard seed**
1     **teaspoon celery seed**
1     **teaspoon mixed pickling spice**
½     **teaspoon ground turmeric**
½     **teaspoon ground ginger**

1. In a large nonmetal container, cook cabbage, onions, peppers, tomatoes, and salt over medium heat until softened, about 10 minutes. Remove from heat, cover, and let stand overnight. Drain and rinse; drain again.

2. In a large sauce pot, stir together mustard and 3 tablespoons vinegar until combined. Add sugar, spices, and remaining vinegar to the pot. Simmer over medium-low heat for 20 minutes. Add vegetable mixture; simmer for 10 minutes more.

3. Ladle mixture into hot jars, filling to ½-inch from top, making sure vinegar solution fully covers vegetables. Wipe rim of jars. Cover with 2-piece lids. Process for 5 minutes in a boiling water bath in canner. Let cool completely on a wire rack or dish towel.

*Our dear friend Wayne Dingus*

I have two car club buddies I have given Chow Chow to every year. One is Wayne Hamilton, and the other was Wayne Dingus. We lost Wayne Dingus a few years ago to cancer. He was a wonderful friend to me and Frank. We still have his wife Sherry, who is a very dear friend. We're thankful to have some really good friends.

# Blackberry Jam

*This one is a family favorite. My daddy, my grandson, and my brother Jerry have all loved eating it over the years. You just can't go wrong with it.*

*Makes about 4 pints*

**8**     **cups crushed fresh blackberries**
**1**     **(1.75-ounce) package fruit pectin**
**½**     **teaspoon salted butter**
**7**     **cups white sugar**

1. In a large stainless Dutch oven, stir together berries, fruit pectin, and butter.

2. Bring mixture to a full rolling boil over high heat, stirring constantly using a long-handled spoon. Add sugar, stir, and return to a full rolling boil. Boil for exactly 1 minute, stirring constantly. Remove from heat and skim off foam, if needed.

3. Ladle into hot jars, filling to ½-inch from top. Wipe rims of jars. Cover with 2-piece lids. Process jam for 10 minutes in a boiling water bath in canner. Let jars stand at room temperature on a wire rack or dish towel for 24 hours. Check to make sure they are sealed.

## My Brother

My dear sweet brother
I love and miss you so
It was so very hard
To have to let you go

I will miss your phone calls
They meant the world to me
I would love to hear your voice
How happy I would be

I know you are in Heaven
With all our loved ones
Give a big hug
To mommy and my son

Life won't be the same without you
You took a piece of my heart
On that sad day
We had to part

But I know we'll meet again someday
On that beautiful shore
And we will be together
Forever more

I will miss and always love you
Each and every day
But I know you are in God's hands
This I will say:

*Take care Jerry you were the best brother in the whole world.*

*Jerry and me*

Every year when I made this jam, my brother Jerry would call and ask me if I made him some, and he would come over and get a jar or two. We lost him and his wife Joann to COVID in 2021. He was 81 years old. It was hard to make the jam this year because I thought of him while I worked on it. He used to tell me that when it came to jam-making, Smuckers had nothing on me. I know my brother would have been proud of this cookbook.

# Peach-Raspberry Jam

*This is one of my favorite jams to enter in the fairs. I've won a few blue ribbons for it. I took it with me to The Today Show, and they all really liked it.*

*Makes about 4 pints*

3    **cups crushed peeled fresh peaches**

1½   **cups crushed fresh raspberries**

1    **(1.75-ounce) package fruit pectin**

6    **cups white sugar**

1. In a large stainless Dutch oven, stir together peaches, raspberries, and fruit pectin using a long-handled spoon. Bring mixture to a full rolling boil over high heat, stirring constantly. Quickly stir in sugar. Return mixture to full rolling boil and boil for 1 minute, continuing to stir constantly. Remove from heat, and skim foam off the surface.

2. Ladle into hot jars, filling to ½-inch from top. Wipe rims of jars. Cover with 2-piece lids. Process for 5 minutes in a boiling water bath in canner. Let cool completely on a wire rack or dish towel.

This is a recipe I made for the first time in 2018. The Russell County Fair's theme that year was Jamin' at the Fair. The Lebanon Food City held a jam contest, and I entered it. They had a table full of different kinds of jams, and two judges looked at them, tested the seals, and ate some of each with a biscuit. The first-place prize was a blue ribbon and a $100 gift card to Food City. I won first place with this jam, and I've been making it every year since.

# Strawberry Jam

*While you can get strawberries year-round, I like to make this during the summer when strawberries are at their sweetest. I make a few batches to last us through the winter.*

*Makes about 4 pints*

5   **cups fresh strawberries**
1   **(1.75-ounce) package powdered fruit pectin**
7   **cups white sugar**

1. Cut and wash strawberries. Mash berries.

2. Use a dry measuring cup to measure berries and dump them into a large saucepan. Stir in powdered fruit pectin. Bring mixture to a full rolling boil over high heat, stirring constantly. Add sugar to fruit mixture in saucepan. Return mixture to a full rolling boil, and boil for exactly 1 minute, stirring constantly. Remove from heat.

3. Ladle into hot jars, filling to ½-inch from top. Wipe rims of jars. Cover with 2-piece lids. Process for 10 minutes in a boiling water bath in canner. Let cool completely on a wire rack or dish towel.

Frank's mother, Celia, was like a second mother to me. She taught me how to appliqué and make quilts and to cook and can a lot of stuff. She was a special lady and loved her family so much. She also loved the Lord and was an inspiration to me all the years I had her in my life. I miss her so much—the little talks we had about the old days. She had a lot of stories to tell.

# Pickled Beets

*My daddy loved Pickled Beets, and my husband Frank is
a big fan of them, too. I like to make them to share
with family and friends who enjoy them.*

*Makes 3 pints*

**3½ pounds small fresh beets
(about 24)**
**2 cups distilled white vinegar**
**1 cup white sugar**
**2 tablespoon pickling salt**
**6 whole cloves**
**1 cinnamon stick**
**3 medium onions, sliced**

1. Wash beets good and trim. Bring large pot of water to a boil; add beets, and boil until tender, about 20 to 25 minutes. Drain, reserving 1 cup beet liquid. Peel and slice beets.

2. In a sauce pot, stir together reserved beet liquid, vinegar, sugar, and salt until combined. Place whole cloves and cinnamon stick in a cheesecloth bag, and tie bag together. Add bag to pot. Bring to a boil; add beets and onions, and simmer for 5 minutes. Remove spice bag.

3. Pack hot jars with beets. Ladle vinegar solution over beets, filling to ½-inch from top. Wipe rims of jars. Cover with 2-piece lids. Process for 5 minutes in a boiling water bath in canner. Let cool completely on a wire rack or dish towel.

*My parents: Henry and Delia Wright*

# Bread-and-Butter Pickles

*These have always been a favorite of mine. I love the flavor
and can eat several of them at a time. My mommy
always made real good ones.*

*Makes about 8 pints*

2     **pounds pickling cucumbers
(3-5 inches long)**
6     **thinly sliced onions**
2     **cloves garlic**
½     **cup pickling salt**
3     **cups water**
1½ **cups white sugar**
3     **cups distilled white vinegar**
2     **teaspoons mustard seed**
1½ **teaspoons ground ginger**
1     **teaspoon ground turmeric**

1. Wash cucumbers; cut crosswise
into ⅛-inch slices. Combine cucumbers
with onions and garlic in a nonmetal
container.

2. Dissolve salt in 3 cups water; pour
over vegetable mixture. Weigh down
with a plate as large as the container.
Place a large jar of water on plate to
keep vegetables under brine. Let
stand for 2 hours. Remove garlic, drain
vegetables; rinse and drain again.

3. In a large sauce pot, bring sugar and
remaining ingredients to a boil. Add
vegetables to hot vinegar solution, and
bring back to a boil. Reduce the heat to
simmer while packing vegetables into
hot jars.

4. Ladle vinegar solution over vegetables,
filling to ½-inch from top. Wipe rims of
jars. Cover with 2-piece lids. Process
for 5 minutes in a boiling water bath in
canner. Let cool completely on a wire
rack or dish towel.

# Pickled Banana Peppers

*My daddy loved these peppers with soup beans and cornbread. I like to chop them up and put them on homemade pizza. They're good on a lot of things!*

*Makes 8 pints*

| 4 | quarts long red and yellow banana peppers |
|---|---|
| 1½ | cups canning salt |
| 18 | cups water, divided |
| 10 | cups distilled white vinegar |
| ¼ | cup white sugar |
| 2 | tablespoons prepared horseradish |
| 2 | cloves garlic |

1. Cut 2 small slits in each pepper and place in large bowl.

2. Dissolve salt in 16 cups of water. Pour salt mixture over peppers, and let stand for 12 to 18 hours in a cool place.

3. Drain peppers, rinse, and drain again thoroughly.

4. Stir together vinegar, sugar, horseradish, garlic, and remaining 2 cups water in a large sauce pot. Simmer 15 minutes. Remove garlic. Bring liquid to a boil.

5. Pack peppers into hot jars, leaving ½-inch of headspace. Ladle vinegar solution into hot jars over peppers, filling to ½-inch from top. Remove all air bubbles. Wipe rims of jars. Cover with 2-piece lids. Process for 5 minutes in a boiling water bath in canner. Let cool completely on a wire rack or dish towel.

### Blue Ribbon Tip
Depending on where you live, you might not be able to find banana peppers in different colors, but any color will work. Just use what you have!

# Canned Tomatoes

*I saw this in an old cookbook I bought at a car show in Elizabethton, Tennessee. I had never made or tasted it before, so I made some out of curiosity. It was pretty good, but I wanted to change the recipe to my liking. I ended up winning a ribbon for my version.*

*Makes 2 quarts*

4    **pounds tomatoes**
4    **tablespoons bottled lemon juice, divided**
2    **teaspoons table salt, divided**

1. Pick fresh tomatoes free of spots. Wash tomatoes, and drain. Place in a wire basket, and lower into a large sauce pot of boiling water. Blanch for 30 to 60 seconds. Remove, and dip immediately into cold water. Slip off skins, and trim off any green areas. Cut out cores. Cut tomatoes into quarters.

2. Place tomato quarters in a large sauce pot, and add water to just cover them. Boil gently for 5 minutes.

3. Divide lemon juice evenly between 2 hot quart-size jars. Carefully pack hot tomatoes and liquid between both jars, leaving ½-inch of headspace. Add 1 teaspoon salt to each jar. Run a nonmetal spatula between tomatoes and jar 2 or 3 times. Press on tomatoes to remove air bubbles.

4. Wipe rims of jars. Cover with 2-piece lids. Process for 45 minutes in a boiling water bath in canner. Let cool completely on a wire rack or dish towel for 12 to 24 hours.

# Jalapeño Salsa

*Good salsa is something that's always nice to have handy for snacking.
You can add more peppers to make this spicier, but I prefer it mild myself.*

*Makes 3 pints*

| | |
|---|---|
| 3 | **cups chopped tomatoes, peeled and cored** |
| 2 | **cups chopped jalapeño peppers, seeded** |
| 1 | **cup chopped onion** |
| 1 | **cup apple cider vinegar** |
| 6 | **cloves garlic, minced** |
| 2 | **tablespoons chopped fresh cilantro** |
| 1½ | **teaspoons table salt** |
| 1 | **teaspoon dried oregano** |
| ½ | **teaspoon ground cumin** |

1. Prepare jars in hot water.

2. Combine all ingredients in a large sauce pot. Bring to a boil over high heat; reduce heat, and simmer for 10 minutes.

3. Ladle salsa into hot jars, filling to ½-inch from top. Wipe rims of jars. Cover with 2-piece lids. Process for 15 minutes in a boiling water bath in canner. Let cool completely on a wire rack or dish towel.

Blue Ribbon Tip

If you are cutting any hot peppers, you need to wear gloves so that you don't get burned.

# Canned Peaches

*My daddy loved Canned Peaches. He would eat them on a hot, buttered biscuit. Daddy loved anything sweet, and my mommy was such a good cook.*

*Makes about 2 quarts*

**3½ pounds peaches**
**3¼ cups white sugar**
**5 cups water**

1. Wash peaches. Dip in boiling water for 30 to 60 seconds; immediately dip in cold water. Slip off peel. Cut in half; hold peach half in hand, and separate halves. Pit and scrape to remove red fibers. Pack peaches between 2 hot quart-size jars, or 4 hot pint-size jars, cavity side down, layers overlapping.

2. Make a syrup by dissolving sugar into 5 cups water in a medium pot. Keep syrup hot on stove. Ladle hot syrup into hot jars over peaches, filling to ½-inch from top. Remove all air bubbles. Wipe rims of jars. Cover with 2-piece lids. Process pints for 25 minutes or quarts for 30 minutes in a boiling water bath in canner. Let cool completely on a wire rack or dish towel.

# Corn Relish

*This was a recipe I saw in a newspaper years ago. I tried it and liked it pretty good, so I made some changes to make it my own. Don't ever be scared to change up a recipe—sometimes you end up making it even better.*

*Makes about 7 pints*

| | |
|---|---|
| 16 | ears yellow corn, kernels cut off cob |
| 1 | (2.5-pound) head green cabbage, chopped |
| 4 | cups distilled white vinegar |
| 1½ | cups white sugar |
| 1 | cup chopped white onions |
| 1 | cup chopped red bell pepper |
| 1 | cup chopped yellow bell pepper |
| 1 | cup water |
| 2 | tablespoons yellow mustard |

| | |
|---|---|
| 1 | tablespoon table salt |
| 1 | tablespoon ground turmeric |
| 1 | teaspoon celery seed |

1. In a large pot, combine all ingredients; simmer over medium-low heat, uncovered, for 20 minutes, stirring occasionally.

2. Ladle into hot jars, filling to ½-inch from top. Wipe rims of jars. Cover with 2-piece lids. Process for 20 minutes in a boiling water bath in canner. Let cool completely on a wire rack or dish towel.

# Grape Jelly

*This is my favorite to put on a peanut butter and jelly sandwich.
I also cook my Weenies in BBQ Sauce (recipe page 77) in it.
I love recipes that can be used in lots of different ways.*

*Makes about 6 half-pints*

| | |
|---|---|
| **5** | **cups grape juice** |
| **1** | **(1.75-ounce) package fruit pectin** |
| **5** | **cups white sugar** |

1. In a large stainless Dutch oven, combine grape juice and fruit pectin. Bring to a full rolling boil over high heat, stirring constantly using a long-handled spoon. Add sugar, stirring until dissolved. Return mixture to a rolling boil, and boil for 1 minute, stirring constantly. Skim foam if necessary.

2. Ladle into hot jars, filling to ½-inch from top. Wipe rims of jars. Cover with 2-piece lids. Process for 5 minutes in a boiling water bath in canner. Let cool completely on a wire rack or dish towel.

# CHAPTER 2

# Dips & Spreads

Dips and spreads are some of my favorite recipes to make because they're so easy to share with others. You'll also notice that most of these recipes only have a few ingredients and come together pretty quickly. Invite some friends over to play cards or watch a football game on TV and serve one of these dishes. I bet it'll be a hit!

A picnic by the lake with our car club

# Me, Frank, and Our Family

*Frank and me, married one year*

OH, WHERE TO BEGIN? Frank and I met when I was just 16, and he was 20 years old. I would wait for the school bus outside an old convenience store, and he would ride by and see me on his way to work each day. We didn't date long because we knew we were meant to be together. We got married October 10, 1964, in the town of Clintwood, Virginia. We rented a small house in the town of Trammel, Virginia. It was a real nice place to live in then and now. Frank drove a coal truck and made $8 a day. It doesn't seem like a lot, but back then it was. I took care of our home and his father, who lived with us—he was like a second father to me. I couldn't cook at all when we first got married. But Frank was sweet and would try to eat whatever I made, usually sandwiches at first. I packed them in his lunch pail every day for him to take with him to work, along with his bottle of Pepsi. One night, my brother, who lived nearby, came over for dinner, and I made biscuits. He couldn't eat them they were so bad, so he tried to feed them to the dog—but the dog wouldn't eat them either. I knew I needed to learn how to cook, so I just kept practicing. The Thanksgiving after our oldest was born, I tried to cook my first turkey. I didn't know you were supposed to take out the package of innards before roasting it, so I left it in. Frank didn't say anything bad about it. I had a lot to learn! My mother taught me some things, but then she passed away. My mother-in-law really stepped in and became like a second mother to me. She taught me how to cook a lot. She told me one time she'd never try to take the place of my mother but that she'd always be there if I needed her. They both meant a lot to me.

*Frank and me posing for family portraits*

*Me and Frank, 1989*

Frank and I had our first child and named him Frank, Jr. He was so cute, with blond hair and blue eyes. We spoiled him, but he was always a good child. He loved school and building model car kits—he was real good at that. He was a son to be proud of. He married the love of his life, Lisa Dean, and they were married 26 years and had a beautiful daughter named Franki. He worked hard and was a wonderful husband and father. We lost him nine years ago. He was killed in a work accident. It was the hardest thing our family has had to go through. He had just become a

*Jane (Frank's sister) and Frank*

*Cathy and Jr. on Easter, 1971*

minister at our church and was going to be ordained. I know he is in Heaven, and I can see him again someday—and that helps. Nothing ever takes away the pain—any one of you who has lost a child knows how we feel. He has two handsome grandsons he never got to meet, but we tell them about their Papaw. He would have loved them so much. I thank God for every day that I had with him, and a piece of our hearts will always be broken. I love you, Jr., and miss you every day.

We had our second child, a daughter, named Cathy, later. She loved her big brother so much, and they were close. They would argue with each other, but no one else could say anything to them. They would always take up for each other. Cathy loved to read and loved horses and any kind of animal. She was a tomboy and wanted to do everything her brother did. She would cry to go to school with him. She met the love of her life, Jerry Johnson, 12 years ago. She was so happy with him. He was a wonderful man and a good husband to her. They both retired and were planning on growing old together. He got COVID-19 in October of 2021, and we lost him. It was so hard on her. She has a dog named Lucy and several cats she rescued, and they keep her busy. She spends a lot of time with us and the rest of the family.

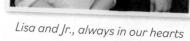

*Lisa and Jr., always in our hearts*

*Cathy's birthday in her 30s at my house*

Later in life, we had our third child, Elizabeth. We all spoiled her. We spent a lot of time playing outside and in our pool. She did a lot of stuff at school, and we did lots of things together. She and I taught children's classes at our church. She is a daddy's girl. She liked school pretty good and did real well. She had lots of pets growing up. Our favorite show to watch when she was little was *Winnie the Pooh*. She graduated from school and met her husband. They have been married 16 years and have five children. She is a wonderful mother, and her husband is a great dad. We are so blessed, and we get to see the grandchildren at least once a week. They are a joy to be with, and it amazes me how fast they are growing.

*Elizabeth and Frank,
a special love*

*Lisa, Jr., Cathy, Frank, me,
and Elizabeth*

# Pimento Cheese Spread

*I came up with this ingredient combination. I love spreading it on sandwiches for everyone to eat when we play cards on Saturday nights.*

*Makes 4½ cups*

2    **cups shredded pepper jack cheese**
2    **cups shredded mild Cheddar cheese**
2    **cups grated Velveeta cheese**
1    **(7-ounce) jar pimentos, drained**
¾    **cup mayonnaise**
1    **teaspoon garlic salt**
1    **teaspoon table salt**
1    **teaspoon ground black pepper**
**Sandwich bread or crackers, to serve**

1. Mix all ingredients together in a bowl until combined. Serve as a sandwich spread or with crackers.

## Resolutions to Live by

Live simply.

Give hope and warmth as you go.

Treat every soul as your own.

Live humbly.

Laugh a lot—write and visit often.

Treat both poor and rich the same, both need love.

Fight ignorance not with darkness, but with light.

Marvel at the stars, they're God's creation.

Play with children, they keep you young.

Hold grudges against no one.

Think deeply and forgive others.

Walk daily in the fields and woods.

Stay learned and well-read, especially the Bible.

Above all, be compassionate and forgiving and kind.

Frank's mother, Celia, made this beautiful quilt many years ago. We keep it on a bed in our house and remember her love.

# Southwestern Dip

*Everyone loves this recipe. You can add or take away any of the ingredients depending on what you like best. I love how colorful it is—it looks real pretty on the table.*

*Makes 6 cups*

| | |
|---|---|
| 1 | (15.25-ounce) can corn, drained |
| 1 | (15-ounce) can black beans, rinsed and drained |
| 1 | cup Italian dressing |
| 2 | green bell peppers, chopped |
| 1 | pint cherry tomatoes, roughly chopped |
| ¾ | cup red onion, roughly chopped |
| 1 | teaspoon ground cumin |

**Tortilla chips, to serve**

1. Mix corn, beans, dressing, bell peppers, tomatoes, onion, and cumin in a medium bowl. Serve with tortilla chips.

Love is limitless! The more you give, the more you have to give. If we love those whose lives we touch each day, they will feel it and pass it on. 1 John 4:8 says, "God is love." This is the way He manifests Himself on Earth. With God's help we can truly love one another as He commands us to do. Spend some time every day reading God's word and praying.

# Strawberry Dip

*I have been making this recipe for a long time. It's a sweet dip and is best when strawberries are in season.*

*Makes 2½ cups*

| 1 | pint (12 ounces) fresh strawberries, trimmed and chopped |
|---|---|
| 1 | (8-ounce) package cream cheese, softened |
| 2 | tablespoons honey |
| 1 | teaspoon vanilla extract |

**Graham crackers, to serve**

1. In a large bowl, beat strawberries, cream cheese, honey, and vanilla together with hand mixer at medium speed for 1 minute. Serve with graham crackers.

*Me and Frank at The Huckabee Show*

❧ I'm going through cancer treatment; I know the Lord has His hands on me. I'm hoping for the best. I have a wonderful team of doctors and the support of my family. I am blessed. ❧

## Life's Blessings

Life is full of trials
We have to go through
But also we have many blessings
Given to me and you

Count the ways you are blessed
Name them one by one
You may take awhile
But it can be fun

Every day we are given
By the Lord above
We should show kindness
Forgiveness and most of all love

If we have a home to sleep in
And food on our table to eat
And family to love us
Life is so sweet

If we have clothes to wear
And shoes upon our feet
These are blessings
That can't be beat

If you're going through a sickness
And you think no one cares about you
Just sit and think again
The Lord cares and I do, too

# Pineapple Cheese Ball

*This cheese ball surprises everyone with its flavors.*
*People don't expect the pineapple, but they always enjoy it.*

*Makes 1 (13-ounce) ball*

**2**   **(8-ounce) packages cream cheese, softened**
**1**   **(8-ounce) can crushed pineapples, drained**
**2**   **cups chopped pecans, divided**
**¼**   **cup chopped green bell pepper**
**2**   **tablespoons chopped onions**
**1**   **tablespoon seasoned salt**
**Crackers, to serve**

1. In a large mixing bowl, combine cream cheese, pineapples, 1 cup pecans, bell pepper, onion, and salt, and shape into 1 large ball or 2 small balls. Refrigerate for 30 minutes.

2. Roll ball in remaining 1 cup pecans, and wrap in plastic wrap. Keep refrigerated until ready to serve. Serve with crackers.

One of my dear friends gave me this recipe in 1983 when we moved to Castlewood, Virginia. June Cassell was her name. She has since passed away, but I will always remember her. She was a great cook who loved to make things for her family.

*Blue Ribbon Tip*
To keep your hands clean, place the mixture onto a piece of plastic wrap to shape into a ball.

# Taco Dip

*Everyone loves this recipe! It's easy to transport and great for taking to a church potluck or to a friend's house.*

*Makes 6 cups*

1 **pound ground beef**
1 **(1-ounce) package taco seasoning mix**
1 **(16-ounce) can refried beans**
1 **(8-ounce) jar tomato salsa**
1 **(8-ounce) carton sour cream**
1 **(8-ounce) package shredded Mexican cheese blend**
**Tortilla chips, to serve**
**Garnish: chopped fresh cilantro**

1. Preheat oven to 325°.

2. In a large skillet, cook beef over medium-high heat until browned. Drain off fat and add taco seasoning to the beef, stirring until well blended.

3. In a 9x9-inch baking dish, layer beef mixture, beans, salsa, sour cream, and cheese.

4. Bake for 15 minutes. Serve warm with tortilla chips. Garnish with cilantro, if desired.

Virginia senator Mark Warner met with me after I gained attention in the summer of 2022. He gave me a nice letter, and we exchanged recipes—he gave me the recipe for his Tuna Melt, and I gave him my Twinkie Surprise. I gave his recipe a try!

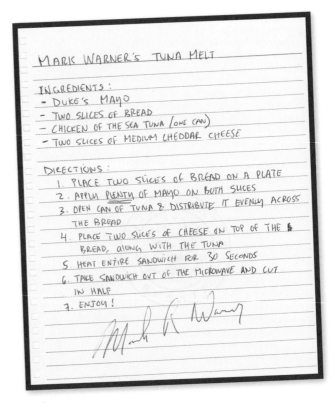

MARK WARNER'S TUNA MELT

INGREDIENTS:
- DUKE'S MAYO
- TWO SLICES OF BREAD
- CHICKEN OF THE SEA TUNA (ONE CAN)
- TWO SLICES OF MEDIUM CHEDDAR CHEESE

DIRECTIONS:
1. PLACE TWO SLICES OF BREAD ON A PLATE
2. APPLY PLENTY OF MAYO ON BOTH SLICES
3. OPEN CAN OF TUNA & DISTRIBUTE IT EVENLY ACROSS THE BREAD
4. PLACE TWO SLICES OF CHEESE ON TOP OF THE BREAD, ALONG WITH THE TUNA
5. HEAT ENTIRE SANDWICH FOR 30 SECONDS
6. TAKE SANDWICH OUT OF THE MICROWAVE AND CUT IN HALF
7. ENJOY!

# Dip for Fries

*Ketchup is always good with French fries, but if you want
something a little special, give this recipe a try.*

*Makes 2 cups*

1    (1-ounce) package ranch
     dressing mix*
1    cup whole buttermilk
1    cup mayonnaise
**French fries, cooked, to serve**

1. In a small mixing bowl, stir together ranch
dressing mix, buttermilk, and mayonnaise.
Refrigerate for at least 2 hours before serving.
Serve with warm French fries.

*\*I use Hidden Valley Ranch Dressing Mix for this recipe.*

# Bacon Broccoli Cheese Ball

*This appetizer looks impressive but is really easy to make. The flavors of cheese and broccoli mixed with bacon are a hit every time.*

*Makes 1 (15-ounce) ball*

1    **(8-ounce) package cream cheese, softened**

1    **cup (4 ounces) shredded mild Cheddar cheese**

½    **teaspoon ground black pepper**

1    **cup finely chopped fresh broccoli florets**

6    **slices bacon, cooked and crumbled**

**Buttery round crackers, to serve***

1. In a bowl, beat cream cheese, Cheddar, and pepper with a hand mixer on medium speed until combined. Stir in broccoli. Shape into a ball. Roll in bacon, and refrigerate, covered, until ready to serve.

*\*I serve this with Ritz crackers.*

# CHAPTER 3
# Appetizers & Snacks

These are some of my most-requested appetizer and snack recipes by family and friends for Christmas and other holidays. I like to make things that are easy for people to pick up and eat while they talk to each other. The most fun things about getting together are eating and enjoying the company.

I love to decorate the mantle for Christmas

Franki and Elizabeth on Christmas day

# Crafting, Baking & Canning

*A favorite birdhouse craft*

I ENTERED MY FIRST FAIR IN 1983. My son, Frank Jr., encouraged me to enter. He was entering model cars in the Russell County Fair that year. He thought I should enter a set of pillow cases I'd embroidered. I told him I didn't have a chance of winning, but he said I should enter anyway. I won first place! I got excited about it, and every year I added a little more. A couple of years into it, I added my baking and canning. I've always enjoyed it, but I sure never thought it'd take off like this!

When I went viral in the summer of 2022 (I didn't even know what that meant at the time!) for winning so many ribbons at the Virginia-Kentucky District Fair, I was shocked. I had been doing this for decades! It's been fun to get a little bit of attention, but one thing I'm really glad about is the focus being put on county fairs again. Entering crafts, baked goods, and canned goods into competitions is good for a person's creativity, and the fairs themselves are great for the communities. I love going to the exhibition halls and walking around to see what everybody else entered. I see friends there, and we congratulate each other on our hard work. It's nice to have these community events that come back year after year.

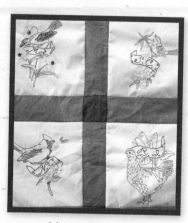
*My state bird quilt*

*A cast-iron pan I painted*

*My jalapeño salsa that won 1st place*

## The County Fair

For a week every year
The county fair rolls into town
Lots of food and rides
Can be found

The smell of all the foods
Quickly fill up the air
You can enjoy all of them
At the county fair

Children shouting happily on rides
As they go up and down
And some go sideways
And others go round and round

Some people are competing
With canning and art and baking
There will be ribbons
For the taking

I love to watch the horse show
Beautiful horses going round
and round
Putting their hooves up
And then touching the ground

No matter what you like
The games, food, or the rides
You can have a lot of fun
With all the things inside

# County Fair Tips

FOR THE LAST 30 YEARS, I've had a lot of good times entering the fair. I love to do it and will continue to as long as I am able. If you have wanted to enter but felt like you weren't good enough or didn't know how, I want to encourage you to. When I entered my first fair, I had no idea I would get a ribbon, but now, I have 1,400. You never know what will happen if you don't try.

I'm still new to social media, but I've enjoyed watching people get excited about county fairs again. They have been a big part of my life, and I love seeing young people entering their work. One girl, Victoria, shared how she wasn't much of a baker, but she was inspired by me to enter her chocolate cake into her local fair. She ended up winning a blue ribbon. I'm real proud of her. My hope is that more people do the same. I gathered my top 3 tips for entering, and I hope these help you start your fair journey.

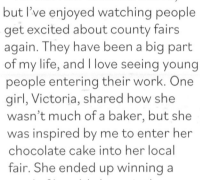

*Needlepoint on plastic*

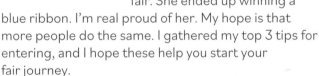

*A farm animal needlepoint on plastic—it won me a blue ribbon!*

First, before deciding what to enter, you need to contact your local fair to get a list of rules and categories. You can even go online and get it off the fair's website. There are a lot of options, and it can be overwhelming for someone new. I'd recommend starting with only a few entries.

Second, your friends and family are the perfect testing audience! I try out new baking things on my loved ones, getting suggestions on what they like. It helps me get my recipes perfect before I bring them to the judges.

Third, no matter what you make, take time to plan out your entries in advance. I pick out crafts I want to enter in the fall and work on them in the winter. Then, come spring and summer, I do all my canning. The last things I work on are my baked goods. Two days before the fair, I do a big grocery shop and buy all my ingredients, then bake up a storm.

I hope this helps some of you get started on your fair journey. It's a great feeling seeing those ribbons on your stuff. It's a lot of work, but it's worth it to know someone else enjoyed it.

*My blue ribbon peanut butter fudge*

*Opposite page: Some of my favorite quilts I've worked on over the years*

# Cornflake Clusters

*I have been making these for about 40 years. They are easy and real good. I've won ribbons with them, and I used to make them for the church social.*

*Makes about 42*

1     **cup light corn syrup**
1     **cup white sugar**
4     **cups cornflakes**
2     **cups creamy peanut butter**

1. Put syrup and sugar in a pot over medium-high heat. Bring to a boil, and let boil for 1 minute. Remove from heat. Add cornflakes and peanut butter. Mix until all the ingredients are fully incorporated.

2. Drop clusters by a heaping tablespoonful onto wax paper. Allow to set for several hours on the countertop before serving.

I used to make these for my two dear friends Lucille and Gilmer Bolinsky. They loved them, so every Christmas, I would make them a tin full. They have both passed away, and I dedicate this recipe to them.

# Ham Rolls

*I always make Ham Rolls on Christmas Eve at my house. Everyone loves them, and they're usually all eaten up. These are also great for tailgating or picnics.*

*Makes 12*

**1**    **(12-ounce) package Hawaiian rolls\***
**1**    **(16-ounce) package sliced ham**
**1**    **(6-ounce) package sliced Swiss cheese**
**¼**    **cup butter, melted**
**1½**  **teaspoons yellow mustard**
**1**    **teaspoon onion flakes**
**½**    **teaspoon poppy seeds**
**½**    **teaspoon Worcestershire sauce**

1. Remove rolls from the packaging but do not separate. Cut all rolls in half lengthwise at the same time. Place ham and cheese on bottom half of rolls. Replace the tops. Place in a 11x7-inch baking dish.

2. Mix together butter, mustard, onion flakes, poppy seeds, and Worcestershire. Pour mixture on top of rolls. Cover with foil, and refrigerate overnight.

3. Preheat oven to 350°.

4. Bake rolls until heated through, 15 to 20 minutes. Serve warm.

*\*I use King's Hawaiian Rolls for this recipe.*

# White Chocolate Peanut Butter Crackers

*I've been making these for 25 years, and they are my daughter Elizabeth's favorite. You can dip them in dark chocolate, but we like white chocolate best. They are easy to make and always good.*

*Makes 12*

**1**     **cup creamy peanut butter**
**24**    **buttery round crackers***
**2**     **cups white chocolate chips**

1. Spread peanut butter on half of crackers, and top with a second cracker.

2. In the top of a double boiler, melt white chocolate chips, and dip cracker sandwiches into it, coating completely. Place on waxed paper to set.

*\*I use Ritz crackers for this recipe.*

Elizabeth and I both love anything with peanut butter. She also loves my Peanut Butter Pinwheel Fudge. When she was growing up, she called it "snake candy" because of how it spirals. Be sure to get your kids and grandkids in the kitchen with you—you'll have wonderful memories!

*Me and Elizabeth*

# Veggie Bars

*A dear friend of mine, Addriene Robinson, gave me this recipe back in about 1992. We taught classes at our church, and she made these. I've been making them ever since.*

*Makes 12*

1     **(8-ounce) can crescent rolls**
2     **(8-ounce) cartons sour cream**
½     **cup mayonnaise**
1     **(1-ounce) package ranch dressing mix***
1     **bunch fresh broccoli, grated**
2     **carrots, peeled and grated**
1     **(8-ounce) package shredded mild Cheddar cheese**

1. Preheat oven to 375°.

2. On a large rimmed baking sheet, press crescent rolls into a 15x11-inch rectangle, and bake for 10-13 minutes. Let cool completely.

3. In a bowl, mix together sour cream, mayonnaise, and ranch dressing mix. Spread mixture onto cooled crescent rolls. Sprinkle broccoli and carrots onto sour cream mixture. Sprinkle cheese on top, and chill for 1 hour. Cut into 12 squares and serve.

*\*I use Hidden Valley Ranch Dressing Mix.*

# Cheese-Stuffed Jalapeños

*This recipe takes a little bit of work, but it's worth it! These are great for when friends and family come over to watch a football game or cookout.*

*Makes 24*

12     **medium jalapeño peppers**
4      **ounces cream cheese, softened**
1      **cup finely shredded mild Cheddar cheese**
½     **cup finely shredded pepper jack cheese**
¾     **teaspoon Worcestershire sauce**
2      **bacon strips, cooked and crumbled**

1. Preheat oven to 400°. Lightly grease a baking sheet.

2. Cut jalapeños in half lengthwise. Remove seeds and membranes. Wash the peppers in a large bowl. Place them in a large saucepan, add water to cover. Bring to a boil for 5 minutes. Drain, and rinse in cold water; set aside.

3. In a bowl, beat cream cheese, cheeses, and Worcestershire with a hand mixer on medium speed until well blended. Spoon 2 teaspoonfuls into each pepper half; sprinkle with bacon. Place on prepared pan.

4. Bake until cheese is good and melted, 5 to 10 minutes. Serve warm.

# Sausage Balls

*One good thing about this recipe is how many sausage balls it makes. It's enough for a crowd, but even still, there usually aren't any left! I make them for my family on Christmas Eve and take them to church dinners.*

*Makes 80*

3    **cups all-purpose baking mix***
1    **pound pork sausage**
2    **cups grated mild Cheddar cheese**
½    **cup grated Parmesan cheese**
½    **cup whole buttermilk**

1. Preheat oven to 350°. Lightly grease a baking sheet.

2 Using your hands, mix all ingredients in a large mixing bowl until well combined. Shape into 80 (1-inch) balls. Place on prepared pan.

3. Bake until golden brown, 20 to 25 minutes. Serve hot.

*I use Bisquick Baking Mix for this recipe.*

*I enjoy growing flowers. This sunflower got as tall as the house!*

### Seasons

When the flowers are blooming
In the spring
The sky is full of birds
Beginning to sing

In the summertime of the year
The gardens are starting to grow
How I love all the vegetables
They taste great you know

When the rain is coming down
And the sun starts to shine
You can see God's rainbow
They are so divine

In the fall of the year
Leaves are falling down
You can feel the chill in the air
Smile at it, don't you frown

Along comes winter, brr
It's starting to turn cold
Put on your coats, build a snowman
And be bold

All these seasons above
Are a gift to us from God alone
We need to thank Him
When all is said and done

# Dilly Pretzels

*This is a great snack that can be made real quick. I like to have these out to share on nights when we're playing cards with friends.*

*Makes 8 cups*

1    **(16-ounce) bag miniature pretzels**
½    **cup vegetable oil**
1    **(1-ounce) package ranch seasoning mix***
½    **teaspoon lemon pepper seasoning**
½    **teaspoon garlic powder**
½    **teaspoon dill**

1. Preheat oven to 350°.

2. Spread pretzels onto an ungreased 15x10-inch baking sheet.

3. Mix together oil, ranch dressing mix, lemon pepper seasoning, garlic powder, and dill weed in a bowl. Pour over pretzels, and mix well.

4. Bake for 14 minutes, stirring every 5 minutes. Let cool completely, and store in airtight container.

*I use Hidden Valley Ranch Dressing Mix.*

 Celia is the one who taught me how to quilt. I remember the first time we sat down together. She was showing me how to stitch the fabric properly, and I thought I was doing a good job. Then, I tried to lift the project up, only to find I had sewed it to my skirt! We had a good laugh about it, and I learned from it. Even though she wasn't family by blood, she loved me like I was her own and taught me a whole lot.

*My current quilting project with each of the 50 state birds*

# Sausage Pinwheels

*I found the inspiration for this recipe in an old cookbook a few years back. You can use hot sausage if you like spicy stuff. I tend to stick to the mild kind, but either way, they are good.*

*Makes 24*

1     **pound mild breakfast sausage**
1     **(8-ounce) package cream cheese, softened**
1     **teaspoon ground mustard**
½     **teaspoon dried dill**
2     **(8-ounce) cans crescent rolls, divided**

1. Preheat oven to 350°.

2. In a large skillet, cook sausage over medium-high heat until browned, and drain well. Mix with cream cheese, mustard, and dill. Lightly grease a baking sheet.

3. Spray wax paper with cooking spray, and place 1 can of crescent rolls on wax paper. Connect the pieces to make a rectangle. Repeat to make a second rectangle. Spread sausage mixture evenly onto both rectangles.

4. Starting with the long side, lift the end of wax paper, and roll up like a jelly roll. Cut each roll crosswise into 12 (1-inch) slices. Repeat to make a second rectangle, using remaining 1 can of crescent rolls. Place on prepared baking sheet.

5. Bake until golden brown, about 20 minutes.

# Weenies in BBQ Sauce

*This is a Christmastime favorite, but I've also made it for church functions or when we have friends over to play cards. I always have to double the recipe because everybody loves them.*

*Makes 10 to 12 servings*

| | |
|---|---|
| 2 | **(28-ounce) packages Lit'l Smokies sausages** |
| 1 | **(18-ounce) bottle barbecue sauce** |
| 1 | **(18-ounce) jar Grape Jelly (recipe page 39)** |

1. Place all ingredients in a slow cooker. Give everything a good stir, cover and cook on high heat for about 2 hours, or until heated through.

# CHAPTER 4

# Soups & Salads

🥄 *Some of the dishes in this chapter are my favorite to take to church dinners and fundraisers. It's pretty easy to make large quantities of these recipes, so it's easy to share with a crowd. The soups are also some of my family's favorite comfort foods— they'll keep you warm on chilly days.*

*Winter when the snow got up to the top of the swimming pool*

*Fall in the mountains*

# Fall in Virginia

AUTUMN IS ONE OF MY FAVORITE seasons. Around here, the leaves change to beautiful colors. When you look off our front porch, you're looking directly at the Appalachian Mountains. The trees paint a pretty picture as far as the eye can see. I love decorating my front porch with fall crafts. I enter some new ones in the fairs every year, and then after the fairs, the crafts are ready to go on the porch. I'm always trying to come up with new ideas for things to create. I think pumpkins, witches, and ghosts are all a lot of fun—so I decorate big for Halloween. I love waiting outside for trick-or-treaters to come by and visit in their cute costumes.

*A fall craft basket that won a 2nd place ribbon*

*A scarecrow I painted*

*A Halloween craft made out of an old bed spring*

*A black cat hat I painted and decorated*

*Autumn leaves around the train track
in my hometown of Dante, Virginia*

## Fall

The leaves are falling down
All over the ground
They make a beautiful sight
Reds, yellows, orange, and brown

You can feel a change in the air
Old Man Winter isn't far away
So get outside and enjoy yourself
Each and every day

You can see pumpkins everywhere
Some are carved out in a design
While others are lit up
There are many different kinds

Soon children will be trick-or-treating
Knocking on your door
Wanting lots of candy
That you bought at the store

There will be witches and ghosts
And goblins and black cats
They are all so cute
Even the little bats

Give them lots of candy
And send them on their way
It will end too quickly
On Halloween day

*Me on my front porch with my fall crafts, waiting for trick-or-treaters*

# Broccoli Cheese Soup

*If you like broccoli, you will really enjoy this soup. It's so creamy
and comforting—it's perfect for cold winter days.*

*Makes about 11 cups*

4    cups water
2    cups potatoes, peeled and diced
2    (10-ounce) packages frozen
     chopped broccoli, thawed
1    cup diced onion
2    chicken bouillon cubes
2    (10.5-ounce) cans cream of
     chicken soup
1    pound Velveeta cheese, cubed
**Rolls and butter, to serve**

1. In a large Dutch oven, bring 4 cups water, potatoes, broccoli, onion, and bouillon cubes to a simmer over medium heat. Cook until potatoes and broccoli are tender, about 8 to 10 minutes. Add soups and cheese, stirring until cheese is melted. Simmer on low heat for 15 minutes. Serve with rolls and butter.

I love working puzzles. I started doing it even more when we were distancing from family and friends during the COVID-19 pandemic. After I finish a good puzzle, I like to frame it to hang as artwork in my house.

# Beef Stew

*My son, Frank Jr., used to love this stew. I made it when he was in high school, and he loved to eat biscuits with it. It's very filling!*

*Makes about 11 cups*

2 tablespoons all-purpose flour
1 tablespoon paprika
2 teaspoons table salt
3 tablespoons plus 1 teaspoon chili powder, divided
2½ pound boneless chuck roast, cut into 1-inch cubes
¼ cup vegetable oil
1 (28-ounce) can diced tomatoes
2 cups red potatoes, peeled and cut into ¾-inch cubes
2 cups carrots, peeled and chopped
2 onions, sliced
1 clove garlic, minced
1 tablespoon ground cinnamon
½ teaspoon crushed red pepper
1 cup frozen peas
**Buttermilk Biscuits (recipe page 187), to serve**

1. In a large bowl or baking dish, mix flour, paprika, salt, and 1 teaspoon chili powder. Add beef and toss to coat.

2. In a large Dutch oven, heat oil over medium-high heat. Cook beef in batches until browned, 4 to 5 minutes per batch.

3. In a 6-quart slow cooker, stir together beef, tomatoes, potatoes, carrots, onions, garlic, cinnamon, red pepper, and remaining 3 tablespoons chili powder. Cover and cook on low heat until tender, 8 to 9 hours. Stir in peas, and serve with Buttermilk Biscuits.

### In Loving Memory of Our Son

*(Rev. Frank A. Skeens, Jr.)*

I'm safely in Heaven now
Though I know you miss me so,
The love I always had for you
Within my heart still flows.

My spirit will remain with you
Every single day,
Appearing as a rainbow or
ocean waves at play.

I'm in the gentle rain that falls
And you feel me in the morning dew.
All that you see that's beautiful reflects my love for you.

# Orange Fruit Salad

*This is my husband Frank's favorite. He likes the mandarin oranges in it a lot. This recipe is good for a fancy lunch or just for eating at home.*

*Makes 8 to 10 cups*

1½  cups cold whole milk
1  (3.4-ounce) package vanilla instant pudding and pie filling
¾  cup sour cream
⅓  cup thawed orange juice concentrate
2  large red apples, chopped
2  (11-ounce) cans mandarin oranges, drained
1  (20-ounce) can pineapple tidbits, drained
1  (15.25-ounce) can tropical fruit, drained
1  (15-ounce) can fruit cocktail, drained

**Garnish: sweetened flaked coconut**

1. In a large bowl, whisk milk and pudding for 2 minutes. Stir in sour cream and orange juice until combined; gently stir in apples, oranges, pineapple, tropical fruit, and fruit cocktail. Cover, and chill in refrigerator for at least 1 hour. Sprinkle with coconut, if desired.

*Beautiful fall leaves in southwest Virginia*

# Chili

*Everybody loves chili. I've been making this for 40 years or more. My family especially loves to eat it when the weather turns cool.*

*Makes about 9 cups*

1  pound ground beef
½  cup chopped onion
1  (16-ounce) can red kidney beans
1  (16-ounce) can refried beans
1  (8-ounce) can tomato sauce
1  cup water
3  tablespoons chili powder
1  tablespoon molasses
1  teaspoon chopped red or green jalapeño
½  teaspoon table salt
½  teaspoon garlic salt
⅛  teaspoon cayenne pepper
**Garnish: shredded Cheddar cheese and sour cream**

1. In a medium Dutch oven, cook beef and onion over medium-high heat until beef is browned. Pour off grease. Add beans, tomato sauce, chili powder, molasses, jalapeño, salt, garlic salt, and cayenne pepper; cover and simmer over medium-low heat for 1 hour, stirring occasionally. Garnish with cheese and sour cream, if desired.

*Blue Ribbon Tip*
This chili is a great topping for hot dogs or baked potatoes.

# Cornbread Salad

*This recipe seems a little unusual to some people, but we've been making it for a long time. It's got a lot of healthy vegetables and some protein. Sometimes I make it to take to a dinner, but I also like to keep it in the refrigerator for easy lunches.*

*Makes 1 (13x9) dish*

1 (10-inch) loaf cornbread, crumbled (7 cups)
3 (16-ounce) cans pinto beans
1 bunch green onions, chopped
1 (15.25-ounce) can corn kernels, drained
1 medium green bell pepper, chopped
1 medium cucumber, chopped
1 medium tomato, chopped
1 (24-ounce) bottle ranch dressing
2 cups shredded Cheddar cheese

1. In a large glass baking dish, layer cornbread, pinto beans, onions, corn, bell pepper, cucumber, and tomato. Repeat, creating a second layer. Add a layer of ranch then sprinkle with cheese. Cover and refrigerate until ready to serve.

This salad was a favorite of my two dear friends Brenda and Oma. We lost both of them to cancer, but they were wonderful cooks and ladies. I always think of them when I make this. My daughter Cathy filmed me making this for social media not too long ago. It was one of my first videos, and it's got over half a million views! Can you believe it? Some people thought I used too much ranch dressing, but I don't think that's possible. My family loves ranch!

# Granny Smith Apple Salad

*A friend gave me this recipe years ago, and I've been making it ever since. The tart fruit tastes make this a good dish for summertime.*

*Makes about 7 cups*

1    **(20-ounce) can crushed pineapple**
⅔    **cup white sugar**
1    **(8 ounce) package cream cheese**
1    **(3-ounce) box lemon gelatin\***
2    **Granny Smith apples, cored and chopped**
1    **(8-ounce) package whipped topping\*, thawed**
1    **cup chopped pecans**
**Garnish: additional chopped pecans**

1. Combine pineapple and sugar in a medium saucepan. Bring to a boil over medium-high heat for 3 minutes. Add cream cheese and lemon gelatin; stir until everything melts together. Let cool completely.

2. In a medium mixing bowl, mix apples, whipped topping, and chopped pecans. Add to cooled pineapple mixture. Let set over night in the refrigerator. Top with extra chopped pecans, if you like. Enjoy!

*\*I like using lemon Jell-O and Cool Whip for this recipe.*

# Potato Soup

*We love eating this Potato Soup in the wintertime with grilled cheese sandwiches and crackers. It is easy to make for a quick family dinner, and I've made it for several fundraisers and dinners at church.*

*Makes about 11 cups*

| | |
|---|---|
| 4 | medium russet potatoes, peeled and cut into 1-inch cubes |
| 4 | tablespoons salted butter |
| 1 | small onion, finely chopped |
| 4 | tablespoons all-purpose flour |
| ¼ | teaspoon crushed red pepper |
| ¼ | teaspoon ground black pepper |
| 3½ | cups whole milk |
| ½ | teaspoon white sugar |
| 1½ | cups shredded Cheddar cheese |
| 1 | cup cubed cooked ham |

**Extra toppings: shredded Cheddar cheese, cooked and crumbled bacon**

1. In a Dutch oven or medium saucepan, add potatoes and cover with water; bring to a boil over medium-high heat. Cook potatoes until fork-tender, about 10 minutes. Drain, reserving 1 cup liquid. Set aside potatoes.

2. In a large Dutch oven or pan, melt butter over medium heat. Add onion, and cook, stirring frequently, until tender but not brown. Add flour, red pepper, and black pepper. Cook for 3 to 4 minutes. Gradually add milk, sugar, cooked potatoes, and reserved cooking liquid. Stir well. Add cheese and ham. Simmer over low heat for 30 minutes, stirring often. Serve with more cheese and bacon, if desired.

# Taco Soup

*I love making this easy recipe for soup dinners at church or for our card nights
with friends. I sometimes make Mexican Cornbread (recipe page 183)
to go with it, and corn chips are good to serve with it, too.*

*Makes about 4 quarts*

| | |
|---|---|
| 2 | **pounds ground beef** |
| 1 | **onion, chopped** |
| ½ | **teaspoon garlic salt** |
| 2 | **cups water** |
| 1 | **(16-ounce) can pinto beans** |
| 1 | **(15.5-ounce) can black beans** |
| 1 | **(15.5-ounce) can kidney beans** |
| 1 | **(15.25-ounce) can yellow corn kernels** |
| 1 | **(14.5-ounce) can diced tomatoes** |
| 1 | **(11-ounce) can white shoepeg corn** |
| 1 | **(10-ounce) can diced tomatoes with green chiles** |
| 2 | **(1-ounce) packages ranch seasoning mix*** |
| 2 | **(1-ounce) packages taco seasoning mix** |

**Tortilla chips**
**Garnish: Cheddar cheese, fresh cilantro, avocado, sour cream**

1. In a large Dutch oven, cook beef, onion, and garlic salt over medium heat until the beef is browned; drain drippings from the pot. Mix in 2 cups water, pinto beans, black beans, kidney beans, yellow corn, tomatoes, shoepeg corn, diced tomatoes with green chilies, ranch dressing mix, and taco seasoning mix. Cook over medium heat for 45 minutes, stirring often. Serve with tortilla chips, and garnish with Cheddar cheese, cilantro, avocado, or sour cream, if you like.

*I use Hidden Valley Ranch Dressing Mix.*

# Chicken Salad

*This has been a favorite on Christmas Eve at my house for a very long time. I serve it on croissants, and everyone loves it.*

*Makes about 5 cups*

3   cups cooked and shredded chicken breast
1   stalk celery, chopped
1   small onion, chopped
4   boiled eggs, peeled and chopped
1   (4-ounce) jar pimentos, drained
1   cup mayonnaise
¼   cup sweet pickle relish
1   teaspoon table salt
¼   teaspoon ground black pepper
Bread, lettuce, sliced tomatoes, to serve

1. In a large bowl, mix together chicken, celery, onion, eggs, pimentos, mayonnaise, pickle relish, salt, and pepper. Cover and refrigerate until ready to serve on bread with lettuce and sliced tomatoes, if you like.

# Pasta Salad

*This has been around a long time, and I like to take it to my family reunion we have every year. One thing I like about it is that you can add any vegetables you like.*

*Makes about 10 cups*

| | |
|---|---|
| 1 | (12-ounce) package tricolor rotini |
| 1 | pint grape tomatoes, halved |
| 1 | cup grated Parmesan cheese |
| 1 | (8-ounce) bottle Italian dressing |
| 1 | green bell pepper, chopped |
| 1 | cucumber, diced |

1. Cook pasta according to package directions, and drain. Place in a large bowl, and add all remaining ingredients, mixing well. Keep in refrigerator until ready to serve.

# CHAPTER 5

# Main Dishes

When Frank and I first got married, I was not a good cook. We had sandwiches for dinner a lot of nights! But over the years, I've learned and gotten better by trying new things. I cook dinner for my family almost every night, and I'm sharing some of my favorite recipes with you. It's important to spend time with your friends and family while eating a good meal as often as you can.

Me on our wedding day

Me and Frank

# Appalachian Living

MY FAMILY IS PROUD TO BE FROM APPALACHIA, southwest Virginia, specifically. When you look out our front door toward the mountains, you can see the holler where Frank was born. My hometown of Dante, Virginia, isn't too far away through the mountains, either. Growing up, we had electricity but didn't always have running water. There weren't ever bathrooms in the house, though. We had big families. I was one of seven, and most people had families with at least that many kids. There wasn't a lot of extra money to go around. We had to grow almost everything we ate. Mommy canned 200 to 300 jars every year.

In our area, everybody either worked in the coal mines or drove trucks. There really weren't any other jobs. To work in a factory, you'd have to move to a bigger town. Most of the men in our families have been coal miners. My daddy used a pick, a shovel, and a lantern light—he worked for $5 a day.

By the time Frank was in the mines, he had an electric light and better equipment. Frank was able to start working when he was only 11 because his sister lied for him. We were thankful for the work, but it was dangerous. My brother, Andrew, worked with Frank in the coal mine. One day, they went to work together, and my brother died. Only Frank came home. They lived next door to us, and it was so hard to lose him. I was always happy when Frank came home in the evenings.

We knew a woman who worked in the mines. She was a single lady and had four young kids. After about a year of working in the mines, she was killed. It was really sad. Back then, there weren't many women who worked in the mines. The guys were nice to her because they knew she needed the money, and she was working hard for it.

In recent years, as the coal mines have closed, people have lost their jobs. Some try to find work doing other things, and a lot of people have had to move. The old coal mining camps are drying up since there's not much work to be found anymore. There's a lot of history around here, and it's still a beautiful part of the country. I enjoy seeing my grandchildren and great-grandchildren growing up in the area.

*The rolling hills of Appalachia*

*My brother Andrew*

*Frank when he was a young boy*

*Some of Frank's mining equipment*

*Opposite page: An old wooden church just outside my hometown of Dante, Virginia*

Dante Coal & Railroad Museum

The house in Trammel I lived in when I met
Frank and we started dating

Frank's garage he built out of an old
barn he tore down

Dante Coal Miners Memorial

The store near where Frank and I first met

A barn outside of Castlewood, Virginia

Opposite page: Frank in his old coal mining helmet

# BBQ Shredded Chicken Sandwiches

*I know everybody's busier these days, and people don't have as much time to cook. This is a slow cooker meal that's easy for busy families during the week. It's nice to stop for a few minutes and spend time with family at the table when you can.*

*Makes about 8 servings*

3    **pounds boneless skinless chicken breast**
1    **teaspoon dry oregano**
¼    **teaspoon ground cumin**
1    **(8-ounce) can tomato sauce**
1    **cup Dr Pepper**
1    **chipotle pepper in adobo sauce**
¼    **cup white sugar**
2    **tablespoons cornstarch**
½    **teaspoon table salt**
2    **tablespoons balsamic vinegar**
**Hamburger buns, potato chips, Bread-and-Butter Pickles (recipe page 29), barbecue sauce, to serve**

1. Place chicken in a 5-quart slow cooker. Season with oregano and cumin.

2. In a bowl, stir together tomato sauce, Dr Pepper, and chipotle pepper. Pour over chicken. Cover and cook on high for 6 hours or low for 8 hours. Move chicken to a bowl. Pour liquid from slow cooker into a small saucepan.

3. In a small bowl, blend sugar, cornstarch, and salt. Stir into saucepan along with slow cooker liquid; add vinegar. Bring to a boil over medium-high heat. Reduce heat, and simmer for 3 minutes until thickened.

4. Shred chicken with 2 forks. Pour sauce over chicken, and stir until mixed. Serve on hamburger buns with Bread-and-Butter Pickles, barbecue sauce, and potato chips.

*Blue Ribbon Tip*
You can add a slice of pepper Jack cheese, if you like, but we love it plain. I like to fix slaw and baked beans to go with it—add a dessert like a banana pudding, and you're done!

# Buffalo Chicken Pizza

*This is a great homemade pizza recipe that's got different flavors than your typical pizza. You can use store-bought crust, so it's quick and easy to put together.*

*Makes 4 servings*

1    pizza crust*
¼    cup ranch dressing
1    cup shredded cooked
     chicken breast
3    tablespoons Buffalo sauce,
     plus more to serve
¾    cup chopped red bell pepper
1    cup shredded mozzarella
     cheese
1    tablespoon grated Parmesan
     cheese

1. Preheat oven to 400°.

2. On pizza pan, place crust. Spread ranch dressing on crust.

3. In a small bowl, stir chicken and Buffalo sauce, and put on crust. Top with bell pepper and cheeses until coated.

4. Place in oven. Bake for 10 minutes or until browned and the cheese is bubbly. Serve with additional Buffalo sauce.

*I use half of 1 (16-ounce) package Mama Mary's Thin & Crispy Gourmet Crust.*

## My Mommy & Daddy

Daddy worked everyday in the coal mine,
A hard way to make
a living back in those days.
He had a wife and seven children
to feed and he always found
the ways.

Mommy cooked for all of us
and kept the house real clean.
Times back then were hard.
They kept their worries unseen.

We went to school everyday
Mommy made sure we did,
She wanted more for us than she
had as a kid.

When we would come home
from school,
She would be cooking our dinner.
It was always so good
She was a winner.

I love them both so much
And miss them every day.
All they did for me
I could never repay.

# Creamy Cheesy Spaghetti

*I got this recipe from my niece, Tiffany, who lives in Indiana. It's kind of a southwestern take on spaghetti or mac-and-cheese, and it's real good. I love sharing recipes with family and friends.*

*Makes about 6 to 8 servings*

8    ounces angel hair or spaghetti pasta
2    (10.5-ounce) cans cream of chicken soup
2    cups diced cooked chicken
2    cups shredded Mexican cheese blend, divided
1    cup salsa
1    cup sour cream
1    tablespoon taco seasoning mix

1. Preheat oven to 350°. Spray a 13x9-inch baking dish with cooking spray.

2. Cook pasta according to package directions, and drain. Put pasta back in pot, and add soups, chicken, 1 cup cheese, salsa, sour cream, and taco seasoning. Stir well to combine. Pour mixture into baking dish. Top with remaining 1 cup cheese. Cover with foil.

3. Bake until hot and bubbly, about 25 minutes.

This is Tiffany's brother and my nephew, Todd Weismann. I was so glad to get to visit with both of them when I went to film for *Huckabee* in Nashville recently.

## The Eagle

An eagle flying across the sky
On this beautiful and sunny day
Not a care in the world
Wish we could be that way

His wings are far apart
As he goes gliding by
Such a beautiful sight
Up in the sky

God made this majestic animal
To watch him fly all around
Thank you Lord
For all the beauty that surround

We can be free like the eagle
When we give God our fears
He will love and protect us
For all of our years

God loves all the animals
Whether they are big or small
But He loves you and me
Most of all

When you are burdened
With worry and pain
Just give them all to God
And peace you will gain

# Slow Cooker Cabbage Rolls

*If you've never made a recipe like this before, it may seem intimidating—but it's really very simple. You just mix everything up and put it in the slow cooker. Before you know it, dinner's ready!*

*Makes 9*

**CABBAGE ROLLS:**

| | |
|---|---|
| 1 | pound ground chuck |
| 1 | cup cooked rice |
| ½ | cup chopped onion |
| ¼ | cup whole milk |
| 1 | large egg, beaten |
| 1 | teaspoon table salt |
| 1 | teaspoon garlic salt |
| ¼ | teaspoon ground black pepper |
| 9 | blanched cabbage leaves |

**SAUCE:**

| | |
|---|---|
| 2 | cups canned stewed tomatoes |
| 1 | (8-ounce) can tomato sauce |
| 1 | tablespoon firmly packed light brown sugar |
| 1 | teaspoon lemon juice |
| 1 | teaspoon Worcestershire sauce |

1. For cabbage rolls: Mix ground chuck, rice, onion, milk, egg, salts, and pepper well. Place ¼ cup mixture on each cabbage leaf, and fold up. Place, seam side down, in a slow cooker.

2. For sauce: Mix together tomatoes, tomato sauce, brown sugar, lemon juice, and Worcestershire. Pour over cabbage rolls. Cover and cook on low for 7 hours.

*Blue Ribbon Tip*
If you cook your whole cabbage head for about five minutes in boiling water, the outer leaves will come off easier for you to stuff them.

# Fried Catfish

*This is Frank's favorite dish. He likes it with slaw, fries, and Hush Puppies (recipe page 175). It can take a while to fry everything up, but it's worth the effort.*

*Makes 10 servings*

1 cup all-purpose flour
1 tablespoon table salt
2 teaspoons ground red pepper
2 teaspoons ground black pepper
1 cup whole buttermilk
1 large egg
2½ cups self-rising cornmeal
1 tablespoon garlic powder
10 catfish fillets
**Oil, for frying**
**Hush Puppies (recipe page 175), lemon wedges, and tartar sauce, to serve**

1. In a shallow dish, mix together flour, salt, red pepper, and black pepper.

2. In a separate bowl, whisk together buttermilk and egg. In a resealable plastic bag, mix together cornmeal and garlic powder.

3. Dredge fish in flour mixture, and dip in buttermilk mixture. Allow excess to drip off. Place catfish in bag with cornmeal mixture, and shake to coat good.

4. Pour oil to depth of 1½ inches in a large cast-iron skillet, and heat over medium heat to 360°. Fry catfish in batches until golden, about 3 minutes on each side. Let drain on paper towels on wire racks. Serve with Hush Puppies, lemon wedges, and tartar sauce.

At one point, after Frank had been working in the mines for years, he hurt himself and had to have surgery. When he went back to work, the mining company forced him into retirement. He worked for a private company for a while, but they didn't want to let him in the mines, which is where the money was. They wanted him to work on the outside in a management position, but he finally convinced them to let him in as a foreman. It was less dangerous than the traditional mining position, but it was higher pay. We were glad about all of that. He eventually retired again, but over the years, he worked just about every job in the coal mines. I'm proud of how hard he's always worked.

# Lasagna

*My daughter Cathy will tell you this is one of her favorite dishes I make.
She likes to have it on her birthday every year! This recipe is also great
to make for large functions at church or with your family.
It's definitely a crowd-pleaser.*

*Makes 6 to 8 servings*

1½   **pounds ground beef**
½   **cup chopped onion**
1   **(14.5-ounce) can whole tomatoes, chopped**
1   **(6-ounce) can tomato paste**
⅓   **cup cold water**
1   **clove garlic, minced**
1   **teaspoon dried oregano leaves, crushed**
¼   **teaspoon ground black pepper**
6   **ounces lasagna noodles, cooked according to package directions**
12   **ounces shredded mozzarella cheese**
½   **pound Velveeta cheese, sliced**
¾   **cup grated Parmesan cheese**
**Breadsticks, to serve**

1. In a large cast-iron skillet, cook ground beef over medium heat until browned; drain. Add onion, and cook until tender. Stir in tomatoes, tomato paste, ⅓ cup water, garlic, oregano, and pepper. Cover and simmer for 30 minutes.

2. Preheat oven to 350°.

3. In a 13x9-inch baking dish, layer half of the noodles, half of meat sauce, half of the mozzarella, half of the Velveeta, and half of the Parmesan. Repeat layers.

4. Bake for 30 minutes. Let stand for 10 minutes before serving.

*I made a castle cake for Cathy's birthday one year*

**Blue Ribbon Tip**

If you have Canned Tomatoes (recipe page 33), you can use a pint here instead of a can from the store. It's even better that way!

# Homestyle Meat Loaf

*I love a meatloaf that's a little sweet from the ketchup, onion, and brown sugar. This one is usually a hit with everyone.*

*Makes 2 loaves*

1½  cups chopped onion (about 1 large onion)
1¼  cups plain dry bread crumbs
¾  cup instant nonfat dry milk
⅔  cup water
½  cup chopped green bell pepper
8  tablespoons ketchup, divided
2  large eggs, beaten
1  tablespoon garlic salt
1  tablespoon dried parsley
1  teaspoon ground black pepper
3  pounds lean ground beef
2  tablespoons firmly packed light brown sugar
1  tablespoon yellow mustard
**Creamed corn, to serve**

1. Preheat oven to 375°.

2. In a large bowl, mix together onion, bread crumbs, dry milk, ⅔ cup water, bell pepper, 2 tablespoons ketchup, eggs, garlic salt, parsley, and black pepper. Add ground beef, and mix well. Divide meat mixture into 2 loaves, and place in an ungreased 13x9-inch baking dish. Flatten loaves on top.

3. Mix brown sugar, mustard, and remaining 6 tablespoons ketchup. Spread on top of loaves.

4. Bake for 55 minutes to 1 hour. Let stand for 10 minutes. Serve with creamed corn.

*Me on my front porch getting ready to cook meat loaf in 1991*

# Pineapple Baked Ham

*Christmas and Easter meals just aren't complete without a Pineapple Baked Ham. Every family has their own sides they like to serve with it, and the good news is that it really goes with anything.*

*Makes 4 to 6 servings*

2    (8-ounce) cans crushed pineapple
⅔    cup firmly packed light brown sugar
1    tablespoon distilled white vinegar
2    teaspoons stone-ground mustard
1    (1-pound) fully cooked sliced ham*

1. Preheat oven to 350°.

2. In a small bowl, mix together pineapple, brown sugar, vinegar, and mustard.

3. Place ham in a 2-quart baking dish. Pour pineapple mixture over ham.

4. Bake for 30 minutes. Serve warm.

*My family loves Kentucky Legend Ham.*

*A ceramic miner I painted*

**Blue Ribbon Tip**
Use any leftover ham to put on biscuits for breakfast. I guarantee those biscuits won't last long!

# Pot Roast

*You can't go wrong with a classic Pot Roast recipe. It's a meal all by itself. Sometimes I cook green beans and rolls to go with it, but you really don't need anything else at all.*

*Makes 6 to 8 servings*

| | |
|---|---|
| 2 | tablespoons vegetable oil |
| 1 | (3½- to 4-pound) boneless chuck roast |
| 1 | (10.5-ounce) can cream of mushroom soup |
| 1 | (2-ounce) package dry onion soup mix |
| 1¼ | cups water, divided |
| 6 | medium russet potatoes, peeled and quartered |
| 6 | carrots, peeled and cut into 2-inch pieces |
| 2 | tablespoons all-purpose flour |

1. In a 6-quart saucepan, heat oil over medium-high heat. Add roast, and brown on all sides, about 2 to 3 minutes per side. Stir in mushroom soup, onion soup mix, and 1 cup water. Put heat on low, cover, and cook for 2 hours.

2. In same pot, add potatoes and carrots. Cover and cook until roast and vegetables are tender, about 45 minutes. Remove roast and vegetables and place on serving platter.

3. In a small bowl, stir together flour and remaining ¼ cup water. Gradually stir into soup mixture. Increase heat to medium-high and cook until mixture boils and thickens, stirring constantly about 2 minutes. Pour over beef and vegetables. Serve immediately.

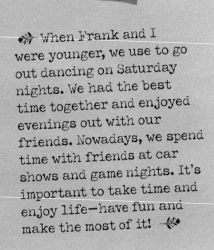

When Frank and I were younger, we use to go out dancing on Saturday nights. We had the best time together and enjoyed evenings out with our friends. Nowadays, we spend time with friends at car shows and game nights. It's important to take time and enjoy life—have fun and make the most of it!

# Salmon Cakes

*My husband loves these, and I've been making them forever because my daddy and mommy liked them, too.*

*Makes 4*

1     **(12-ounce) can salmon, drained**
2     **large eggs, beaten**
10   **saltine crackers, crushed**
**Table salt and ground black pepper, to taste**
2     **tablespoons all-vegetable shortening***
½     **cup mayonnaise**
¼     **teaspoon lemon zest**
1     **tablespoon fresh lemon juice**
¼     **teaspoon table salt**

1. Mix together salmon, eggs, crackers, salt, and pepper. Form into 4 patties.

2. Heat all-vegetable shortening in a cast-iron skillet over medium heat. Add patties, and fry until brown, about 2 to 3 minutes per side. Let drain on paper towels.

3. Stir together mayonnaise, lemon zest, lemon juice, and salt. Serve patties topped with a spoonful of mayonnaise mixture.

*\*I use Crisco.*

*Celia with Elizabeth*

*Blue Ribbon Tip*

My mother-in-law Celia told me to get the Crisco hot in the iron skillet and sprinkle a little meal in it before putting the salmon cakes in to fry. This makes them crispier.

# Sourdough Steak

*This is an old recipe that's got a great flavor to it. I like to serve it with biscuits and mashed potatoes. If you don't currently have a Sourdough Starter, I encourage you to make one. You'll be able to make bread and all sorts of things once you have it.*

*Makes about 8 servings*

| | |
|---|---|
| 1 | **(3-pound) 1-inch-thick round steak** |
| 2 | **cups all-purpose flour** |
| 4 | **teaspoons onion salt** |
| 4 | **teaspoons paprika** |
| 2 | **teaspoons ground black pepper** |
| 1 | **cup Sourdough Starter (recipe follows)** |

**All-vegetable shortening\* or lard**
**Mashed potatoes, green beans (optional), to serve**

1. Using a meat-tenderizing mallet, pound steak to ½-inch thick. Cut into about 8 portions.

2. In a shallow dish, mix together flour, onion salt, paprika, and pepper.

3. Dip steak into Sourdough Starter, then into flour mixture.

4. In a large, deep cast-iron skillet, add shortening or lard to a depth of 1-inch, and heat over medium to medium-high heat. Add steaks in batches, and cook until browned, about 3 minutes per side. Let drain on paper towels. Serve with mashed potatoes and green beans (optional).

*\*I use Crisco.*

**SOURDOUGH STARTER:**

| | |
|---|---|
| 1 | **quart lukewarm water** |
| 1 | **(0.25-ounce) package active dry yeast** |
| 2 | **teaspoons white sugar** |
| 4 | **cups all-purpose flour, plus more as needed** |

1. Pour 1-quart of water into a 3-quart glass or ceramic bowl. Add yeast and sugar to soften. Stir in flour. Cover with a clean cloth.

2. Let rise until mixture is light and slightly aged, about 2 days. Mixture will thin as it ages, so add flour as needed. As you use sourdough from crock, replace it with equal amounts of flour and water. Store in the refrigerator.

One night, we took the kids to a movie. While we were gone, our house burned down. We lost everything, but thankfully the animals got out safely. We praise God no one was injured. Our family lost some special things we couldn't replace, but it was all just stuff. It reminded us that people and our relationships are what truly matter.

# Spaghetti & Meatballs

*My grandkids always request this meal. I love having them over to my house to cook with me or make crafts. We have a great time together.*

*Makes about 6 to 8 servings*

2 teaspoons olive oil
1½ pounds mild Italian sausage links, halved crosswise

**MEATBALLS:**
1 pound ground beef
¼ cup grated Parmesan cheese
9 saltine crackers, finely crushed
¼ cup water
1 large egg
1 teaspoon tomato paste
½ teaspoon table salt
¼ teaspoon ground black pepper
¼ teaspoon dried oregano
¼ cup vegetable oil

**SAUCE:**
¼ cup olive oil
2 ounces thinly sliced prosciutto, chopped
5 garlic cloves, minced
2 (28-ounce) cans crushed tomatoes
1 cup water
Hot, cooked spaghetti and Parmesan cheese, to serve

1. In a large skillet, heat oil over medium heat. Add sausage, and cook, turning frequently, until browned, about 10 minutes. Remove from skillet, and set aside. Wipe skillet.

2. For meatballs: Mix together beef, Parmesan, crackers, ¼ cup water, egg, tomato paste, salt, pepper, and oregano. Shape mixture into 1½-inch balls. In the same skillet, heat oil over medium heat. Add meatballs and cook until browned, about 10 minutes. Let drain on paper towels.

3. For sauce: In a large pot, heat oil over medium heat. Add prosciutto and garlic and cook until garlic is fragrant and turns golden brown, about 2 minutes. Stir in tomatoes and 1 cup water. Add sausage; bring sauce to a simmer, and cook over low heat, about 15 minutes. Scoop out sausage, and transfer to a plate. Cover and keep warm. Add meatballs to sauce, and return to a simmer for 10 minutes more. Add cooked sausage back in sauce. Serve with spaghetti and Parmesan.

**Blue Ribbon Tip**
I like to serve this recipe with a green salad to get some vegetables into the meal.

# CHAPTER 6

# Casseroles

It's always nice to have some tried-and-true casserole recipes in your pocket for church functions and potlucks. And, if you're a southerner, it's nearly a requirement that you master at least a few. These are my favorites—some are side dishes, and some are main dishes. I hope you'll find several to add to your own casserole rotation.

*My church*

# Church & Community

MY DAUGHTER-IN-LAW LISA and I taught Missionettes for 26 years at our Assembly of God church in the next town over (St. Paul, Virginia). Lisa and I would drive the church van and pick up the kids for church. We had classes and teachers for kids ages 3- to 19-years-old. The classes had cute names for each group, like Rainbows, Daisies, and Stars. We taught the kids about the Bible and had snacks and crafts. We made a lot of good friendships over the years, not only with the kids, but with parents and grandparents, too.

*Me and Lisa are very close.*

After my daughter Elizabeth got married, she joined us in teaching Missionettes classes. We had a lot of good teachers like sisters Eva, Kellie, Carol, Lorena, Oma, Anita, and Addrienne—so many sweet ladies—Margaret, too. They all had a heart for God and teaching His word. I enjoyed every minute I had with this church group. Lisa and I also kept the nursery class for 10 years on Sunday mornings during the Sunday School hour. They were all a blessing, too.

I've enjoyed cooking for church programs and functions over the years. For a while, I helped with the funeral dinner program. If someone in the church lost a loved one, a bunch of us ladies would cook a dinner for the family. I also helped three other ladies cook for our seniors in church once a month. We would take the van and pick up everyone and take them to church. We cooked a good meal for them, had a devotion and prayer time, and played bingo. My friends Mary, Peggy, Della, Doris, Shirley, and Gerfus did this with me. They're all very dear friends, and I'm thankful for the time we spent together.

*A Missionette retreat in Ghent, West Virginia. We did this trip every year with our church. (left to right: Lisa, Franki, Elizabeth, Donna, me, and Shelly)*

*Missionette retreat in Ghent, West Virginia. (left to right: Oma, Barbara, Addriene, Elizabeth, Brother Branch, Franki, Lisa, and me)*

*Frank Jr. reading his Bible. He loved his church.*

Our son, Frank, Jr., was going to be ordained as a minister in West Virginia. He passed away before this happened, but he had preached some in our church in St. Paul, Virginia. I know he is with God, and I will get to see him again some day. So many people came to his funeral and told us how special he was to them. It helped hearing how he had touched people's lives. Sometimes it's easy to forget how important your community is to you until you really need them. We're so grateful for the people who've helped support us during hard times. We hope people lean on us when they need us, too.

Faith in God is very important to me. We have trials and we go through lots of things in our lives. We have to give up loved ones, and it hurts. We have sickness, worries, and problems to deal with daily. Knowing God is aware of all this, and He is there to help me and you get through all these times is a blessing. It's good to know we have something better to look forward to when we leave this Earth. Heaven is a place of hope for the saved. Scripture describes it as a beautiful city where we will live forever. There will be singing, worshipping, serving, fellowship with others, and eating. It is a life of fellowship with God—a life of rest, growth, and worship. As Christians, we are gathering friends on Earth to spend eternity with in Heaven. My late son told me one night when we were coming home from church in his Jeep, "Mommy, no one knows when their time on this Earth is up, so we just have to be ready to meet the Lord." I love and miss him so much, but I know he's in good hands with God.

*Needlework on plastic*

# Broccoli Casserole

*My sister-in-law Jane and I both love this casserole. There are a lot of different types of broccoli casseroles, but this one's my favorite. The cheese cracker topping makes this one unique.*

*Makes 6 servings*

| | |
|---|---|
| 1 | cup water |
| ½ | teaspoon table salt |
| 2 | (10-ounce) packages frozen chopped broccoli |
| 1 | onion, chopped |
| 2 | cups shredded sharp Cheddar cheese, divided |
| 1 | (10.5-ounce) can cream of mushroom soup |
| 1 | large egg |
| 1 | cup crushed cheese-flavored crackers* |

1. Preheat oven to 300°.

2. In a medium saucepan, bring 1 cup water and salt to a boil. Add the broccoli and onion. Cover and simmer for 5 minutes. Drain.

3. In a large bowl, mix 1 cup cheese, mushroom soup, egg, and drained broccoli and onion. Place in an 2-quart baking dish. Top with crackers and remaining 1 cup cheese.

4. Bake for 30 minutes.

*I use Cheez-Its.

# Loaded Red Potato Casserole

*If you like twice baked potatoes, you'll love this recipe. It's similar, but it's even easier since everything bakes up together in a casserole dish.*

*Makes 8 servings*

16  small red potatoes, halved or quartered if larger
½   cup whole milk
¼   cup salted butter, cubed
½   teaspoon table salt
½   teaspoon ground black pepper
1½  cups shredded mild Cheddar cheese, divided
½   cup crumbled cooked bacon
1   (8-ounce) carton sour cream

1. Preheat oven to 350°. Grease a 13x9-inch baking dish.

2. In a 6-quart pot, bring potatoes and water to cover to a boil over medium-high heat. Cook, uncovered, until tender, about 15-20 minutes. Drain, and immediately return potatoes to same pot.

3. To the potatoes, add milk, butter, salt, and pepper, gently stirring until butter melts. Spread into prepared pan. Sprinkle with 1 cup cheese and bacon. Dollop the sour cream on top, and sprinkle with remaining ½ cup cheese.

4. Bake, uncovered, until cheese is melted, about 20 minutes.

*Sis and Bobby Skeens*

❧ Sis Skeens, who is married to Frank's cousin, gave me this recipe, and she's a great cook. She cooks a lot like I do, and we love to go out to eat together and talk. She is like a sister to me. ❧

# Enchilada Casserole

*I like that this recipe is simple and doesn't have too many ingredients. It's a great weeknight dinner when you don't have extra time to spend in the kitchen, and it's got flavors everybody loves.*

*Makes 6 servings*

| | |
|---|---|
| 1 | (15-ounce) bag tortilla chips, divided |
| 2 | cups shredded mild Cheddar cheese, divided |
| 2 | cups shredded cooked chicken |
| 1 | (15-ounce) can green chili sauce |
| 1 | (10.5-ounce) can cream of chicken soup |
| 1 | (10-ounce) can enchilada sauce |

1. Preheat oven to 400°. Grease a 13x9-inch baking dish.

2. Arrange a layer of chips on the bottom of prepared pan. Sprinkle 1 cup cheese on top.

3. In a medium bowl, stir together chicken, chili sauce, soup, and enchilada sauce. Pour half of the chicken mixture over the cheese layer. Add another layer of chips, and spread remaining chicken mixture on top. Sprinkle with remaining 1 cup cheese.

4. Bake until bubbly and lightly browned, 20-25 minutes.

# Cabbage Roll Casserole

*This casserole has all the great taste of cabbage rolls, but it doesn't take quite as much effort. It's great for a quick weeknight dinner.*

*Makes 8 servings*

1 tablespoon vegetable oil
1 medium head cabbage, chopped in 1-inch pieces
1 pound lean ground beef
2 tablespoons minced onion
1 tablespoon minced garlic
1 (15-ounce) can tomato sauce
1 (14-ounce) can petite diced tomatoes
¼ cup water
½ teaspoon paprika
**Table salt and ground black pepper, to taste**
2 cups cooked long-grain rice
1 cup shredded Monterey Jack cheese

1. Preheat oven to 350°. Grease a 13x9-inch pan.

2. In a saucepan, heat oil over medium-high heat. Add cabbage, and cook until partially cooked, 7 minutes. Put half of cabbage in greased pan.

3. In a large skillet, cook the beef, onion, and garlic over medium-high heat, until beef is browned. Drain and return to skillet. Add tomato sauce, tomatoes, ¼ cup water, paprika, salt, and pepper to beef mixture. Cover and simmer for 15 minutes, stirring once. Add cooked rice, and heat until warm.

4. Layer half of beef mixture over cabbage in pan. Top with remaining cabbage, and finish with beef mixture on top.

5. Cover and bake for 35 minutes. Take out, uncover, and top with cheese. Bake for 15 minutes more.

Elizabeth, my youngest daughter, first made this for me. I loved it so much that I now make it regularly. Elizabeth is a wonderful cook and mother to five of my grandchildren.

# Super Chicken Casserole

*This is one of my favorite casseroles, and it's hardy enough to be the main dish. I like to serve it with biscuits.*

*Makes 6 servings*

4   cups chopped cooked chicken
1   (10.5-ounce) can cream of chicken soup
1   (8-ounce) carton sour cream
1½  cups chicken broth
1   (6-ounce) package cornbread stuffing mix

1. Preheat oven to 350°.

2. Place chicken in a large baking dish.

3. In a small bowl, mix soup and sour cream. Pour over chicken.

4. In a separate bowl, combine chicken broth and stuffing mix. Spread over casserole.

5. Bake until browned, about 45 minutes.

**Blue Ribbon Tip**

You can boil your own chicken and chop it up for this dish. If you're short on time, you can also buy a rotisserie chicken already cooked from the grocery store or even use canned chicken. Leftover chicken can be used for Chicken Salad (recipe page 98).

# Hashbrown Potato Casserole

*My younger brother Sammy gave me this recipe 20 years ago. My nieces Amy and Hannah and my granddaughter Franki all love it, too. It's a family favorite for Thanksgiving.*

*Makes 8 servings*

| | |
|---|---|
| 1 | (32-ounce) bag diced hashbrown potatoes, thawed |
| 1 | (8-ounce) carton sour cream |
| ½ | pound Velveeta, chopped into cubes |
| 1 | (10.5-ounce) can cream of chicken soup |
| 1 | small onion, chopped |
| ½ | cup salted butter, melted and divided |
| 2 | cups cornflakes cereal, crushed |

1. Preheat oven to 350°. Grease a 13x9-inch baking dish.

2. In a medium mixing bowl, mix potatoes, sour cream, Velveeta, soup, onion, and ¼ cup melted butter together; put into prepared pan.

3. In a separate medium mixing bowl, mix cornflakes with remaining ¼ cup melted butter. Put on top of potato mixture.

4. Bake for 30 minutes.

# Corn Casserole

*This casserole is perfect for a summer barbecue or potluck. It's easy and inexpensive to put together—and best of all, everyone loves it!*

*Makes 6 servings*

1    (8-ounce) package cream cheese
2    cups shredded mild Cheddar cheese
½    cup salted butter
3    tablespoons pickled jalapeño peppers, chopped
3    (11-ounce) cans white shoepeg corn
**Garnish: chopped fresh parsley**

1. Preheat oven to 350°. Grease a 2-quart baking dish.

2. In a medium saucepan, heat cream cheese, cheese, butter, and jalapeños on low heat until cheese melts. Add corn, and tir well. Pour into prepared pan.

3. Bake for 30 minutes. Garnish with chopped parsley, if desired.

## A Beautiful Day

It's a beautiful day outside
The sun is shining so bright
The clouds are rolling by
Such a beautiful sight

The peepers are calling
A sure sign of spring
It makes me so happy
The joy that it can bring

Some flowers are coming up
Still early yet
There will be plenty more
On that you can bet

Every day that I live
Is a blessing from God above
He has shown me kindness
And so much love

Spring is the best time of year
A time of hope and love
A time for renewal
And thanking God above

Stop and smell the roses
Make each day the best you can
Be good to your family
And to your fellow man

# CHAPTER 7

# Sides

Side dishes are an important part of any meal. Most families have certain recipes that they remember always being served at special holidays—my family is that way, too. These are some of our favorite sides. I hope you'll give some of them a try and find a few new recipes to add to your dinner lineup.

Me and Frank riding in our Mustang

Me and Frank in our Roadrunner at a car show. Love those Mopars!

# Car Shows

MY HUSBAND, FRANK, REALLY LOVES OLD CARS. The first car show he went to was back in 1971 with our son, Frank, Jr. A few years later, I started going with him. I enjoy going because we've formed a lot of friendships over the years with other folks who go to the shows. We get to see each other's cars, sit and talk, and eat with each other—it's fellowship. There's usually an entry fee for the car shows, and the money raised goes to charity, typically a children's hospital. We like that we get to participate in these fundraisers that support a good cause.

When Frank retired from the coal company, he got even more interested in cars. He bought an old GTX about 15 years ago and put it back together. That started him on restoring cars. Now he buys a new one every few years, works on it to get it just right, then sells it and starts again. Our daughter, Cathy, enjoys cars, too. She and Frank have traveled all over looking at some of Frank's potential car projects over the years. I am happy that our family has bonded over our love of cars and each other.

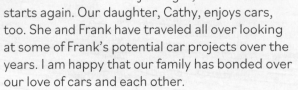

*Frank and his Mach 1 Mustang*

*Cathy with her hellcat*

*At the lake with our Mustang*

*Frank's old car at the garage he built our of a barn*

*Gene and Brenda*

*Cliff and Barbara*

*Me, Joyce, Barb, Sharon, Gerry, and Joetta in a 50s diner
at a car show in Rogersville, Tennessee*

*Darrell*

*Me and Frank riding in our Roadrunner in a Christmas parade*

*Ron and Bonnie*

# Cornbread Dressing

*I've been making this Cornbread Dressing for Thanksgiving dinner for the last 45 years. My mother-in-law, Celia, could make it better than anyone. I think love and care were the special ingredients.*

*Makes 10 servings*

1      pound pork sausage
1½    cups chopped celery
       (include leaves)
1¼    cups chopped onion
5      cups crumbled cornbread
       (about an 8-inch loaf)
4½    cups day-old bread cubes
2      teaspoons rubbed sage
½     teaspoon ground black pepper
3      cups chicken broth
2      tablespoons salted butter

1. Preheat oven to 350°. Grease a 3-quart baking dish.

2. In a large cast-iron skillet, cook sausage over medium heat, stirring frequently, until browned. Remove with a slotted spoon, and let drain on paper towels.

3. In the same skillet with drippings, cook celery and onion over medium heat, until tender, about 15 minutes.

*Frank and Celia*

4. In a large bowl, mix together sausage, vegetable mixture, cornbread, bread cubes, sage, and pepper. Moisten with chicken broth. Put in prepared dish, and dot butter on top.

5. Bake, covered with foil, for 20 minutes. Uncover, and bake until browned, about 10 minutes more.

# Oven-Fried Green Tomatoes

*Everyone loves Oven-Fried Green Tomatoes in the summertime. This recipe is made best with tomatoes straight from the garden, but fresh ones from the market work just fine, too.*

*Makes about 6 servings*

| | |
|---|---|
| 1 | cup yellow cornmeal |
| 1 | cup fresh bread crumbs |
| 1 | teaspoon table salt |
| 1 | teaspoon ground black pepper |
| 2 | large eggs |
| ¼ | cup water |
| 4 | large green tomatoes, cut into ½-inch slices |

1. Preheat oven to 450°. Lightly spray a large baking sheet with cooking spray.

2. In a shallow dish, mix together cornmeal, bread crumbs, salt, and pepper. In another shallow dish, whisk together eggs and ¼ cup water. Dip each tomato slice into egg mixture, and then in cornmeal mixture to coat. Place slices on prepared pan. Spray tops with cooking spray.

3. Bake until golden brown, about 25 minutes.

When I was a teenager, Frank tried to teach me how to drive. We were practicing one day on the mountain roads around southwest Virginia, and I almost drove us off a cliff! The only reason we didn't go over is because Frank quickly cut the car off. The nose of the car was tipped over the edge. It scared me to death! I didn't want to drive again after that, so Frank became my driver. When the kids got older, I rode around with them, too. I like riding in cars and going to shows to look at them, but I don't like driving them!

# Cowboy Beans

*Dried bean dishes have always been important food for Appalachian families. This is one of our favorite ways to cook them.*

*Makes about 10 cups*

| | |
|---|---|
| 1 | **pound dried pinto beans** |
| ½ | **pound salt pork, cut up into 1-inch pieces** |
| 8½ | **cups cold water, divided** |
| 1 | **red chili pepper, seeded and chopped** |
| 1 | **medium onion, chopped** |
| 1 | **(6-ounce) can tomato paste** |
| 1½ | **tablespoon chili powder** |
| 1 | **teaspoon table salt** |
| 1 | **teaspoon cumin seed** |
| 1 | **clove garlic, minced** |

1. Wash and pick over beans, and toss in a large bowl. Cover beans with cold water, and soak overnight.

2. Next morning, drain the beans. In a Dutch oven, combine beans and 6 cups water. Bring to a boil over medium-high heat; reduce heat, cover, and simmer for 1 hour.

3. To the beans, stir in pork, remaining ingredients, and remaining 2½ cups cold water. Cover and simmer until beans are tender, about 2½ to 3 hours.

❧ I wanted to do this puzzle since it has Frank's name on the car garage. He got a real kick out of it, and we thought it was pretty enough to frame after it was put together! ❧

*Blue Ribbon Tip*

Don't forget to plan ahead for this recipe. You'll need to start soaking your beans the night before you want to make this dish.

# Garlic Mashed Potatoes

*This is a side dish that goes with just about anything. Sometimes I serve it with meat loaf and green beans, other times I like it with roast beef, gravy, and Texas toast. You can't go wrong with this one.*

*Makes about 4 cups*

| | |
|---|---|
| 2½ | **pounds russet potatoes, peeled** |
| 1 | **whole garlic head** |
| 1 | **tablespoon olive oil** |
| ½ | **cup sour cream** |
| 2 | **tablespoons salted butter** |
| ⅓ | **cup sliced green onion** |
| ½ | **teaspoon table salt** |
| ¼ | **teaspoon ground black pepper** |

**Garnish: sliced green onions**

1. Preheat oven to 375°.

2. Cut potatoes into even slices. Bring potatoes and lightly salted water to cover to a boil over medium-high heat. Reduce heat, and simmer until the potatoes are tender but still hold their shape, about 20 minutes.

3. In the meantime, separate garlic cloves, but don't peel them. Place garlic in a small bowl, add oil and toss. Place on a small baking pan.

4. Bake for about 10 minutes. Let cool slightly.

5. Drain potatoes, and return to pot. Mash slightly. Add sour cream, butter, and green onion. Quickly squeeze pulp from garlic with potatoes. Add salt and pepper. Mash potatoes until smooth. Garnish with green onions, if desired.

# Parmesan Baked Squash

*The sweetness of the squash combined with the flavors of Parmesan cheese in this baked dish is just so good. I love eating yellow squash when they're in season.*

*Makes 3 to 4 servings*

| | |
|---|---|
| 1 | cup whole buttermilk |
| 1 | cup grated Parmesan cheese |
| ½ | cup all-purpose flour |
| 1 | large yellow squash (about 12 ounces), cut into ½-inch slices |
| ½ | teaspoon table salt |
| ½ | teaspoon ground black pepper |

1. Preheat oven to 425°. Spray a large baking sheet with cooking spray.

2. Place buttermilk in a shallow bowl. Mix cheese and flour in another shallow dish. Dip squash into buttermilk and then toss in cheese mixture to coat well. Place on prepared pan, and sprinkle with salt and pepper.

3. Bake until golden, about 8 to 10 minutes. Turn over, and bake until golden, about 8 to 10 minutes more.

# Golden Parmesan Potatoes

*This is one of the easiest side dishes I make. It takes only a little time to put together, but it's hearty and comforting.*

*Makes 4 to 6 servings*

½    **cup grated Parmesan cheese, plus more to serve**
¼    **cup self-rising flour**
¾    **teaspoon seasoned salt**
6    **1½-inch-chunks peeled russet potatoes (about 4 large potatoes)**
½    **cup salted butter**
**Table salt and ground black pepper, to taste**

1. Preheat oven to 375°.

2. In a large resealable plastic bag, combine cheese, flour, and seasoned salt. Add potato chunks, and shake to coat.

3. Place butter in a 13x9-inch baking pan or dish; place in oven until butter is melted. Put coated potatoes in butter.

4. Bake until tender and golden, about 40 minutes. Sprinkle with salt, pepper, and additional Parmesan to taste.

🌿 The last year since my Leukemia diagnosis has been hard at times, but I have so much to be grateful for. I am especially thankful for the good medical care I've gotten. I take a chemotherapy pill every day and go for regular checkups. Feeling connected to my family and friends along with staying active by cooking and crafting keeps my spirits up. 🌿

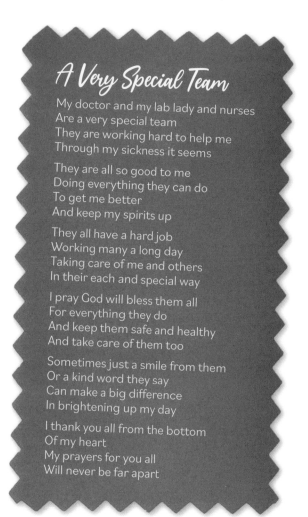

## A Very Special Team

My doctor and my lab lady and nurses
Are a very special team
They are working hard to help me
Through my sickness it seems

They are all so good to me
Doing everything they can do
To get me better
And keep my spirits up

They all have a hard job
Working many a long day
Taking care of me and others
In their each and special way

I pray God will bless them all
For everything they do
And keep them safe and healthy
And take care of them too

Sometimes just a smile from them
Or a kind word they say
Can make a big difference
In brightening up my day

I thank you all from the bottom
Of my heart
My prayers for you all
Will never be far apart

# Mac & Cheese

*Who doesn't love Mac & Cheese? When I worked in the school cafeteria, Mac & Cheese was a favorite. My niece, Hannah, always wants this specific version for Thanksgiving dinner, and the rest of the family loves it, too.*

*Makes about 5 cups*

2¼  **cups elbow macaroni**
8   **ounces Velveeta cheese, cut in cubes**
1   **cup whole milk**
¼   **cup salted butter**
3   **tablespoons firmly packed light brown sugar**

1. Cook macaroni according to package directions, and drain. Return to pot. Add all remaining ingredients, and stir over low heat until Velveeta is melted. Serve warm.

*The school where I worked in the cafeteria— I made wonderful friends there*

*The school Jr. and Cathy attended near Trammel, Virginia, when they were growing up*

# Deviled Eggs

*My grandson puts in a request for Deviled Eggs every chance he gets! And I don't blame him—they're good!*

*Makes 24*

| | |
|---|---|
| 12 | **large eggs, boiled, peeled, and halved** |
| ½ | **cup sweet pickle relish, drained** |
| ½ | **cup mayonnaise** |
| 2 | **teaspoons yellow mustard** |
| 1 | **teaspoon white sugar** |
| ½ | **teaspoon table salt** |
| **Paprika, optional** | |

1. Remove yolks from eggs, and put in a bowl; add relish, mayonnaise, mustard, sugar, and salt. Mix well, and evenly spoon yolk mixture into egg whites. Refrigerate until ready to serve. Sprinkle with paprika, if desired.

# Coleslaw

*This is a great dish for family reunions or other large gatherings. Sometimes I make it for card game nights and serve it with BBQ Shredded Chicken Sandwiches (recipe page 106) and baked beans.*

*Makes about 5 cups*

| | |
|---|---|
| 1 | **medium head cabbage, grated (about 2½ pounds)** |
| 1 | **large carrot, peeled and grated** |
| 2 | **cups mayonnaise** |
| ¾ | **cup white sugar** |
| 3 | **tablespoons distilled white vinegar** |
| 1 | **tablespoon table salt** |
| 1 | **teaspoon ground black pepper** |

1. In a large bowl, combine cabbage and carrot. Add mayonnaise, sugar, vinegar, salt, and pepper. Mix well, and refrigerate until cold, about 2 hours.

# CHAPTER 8

# *Breads*

Some people are intimidated by bread recipes, but I've found they really aren't too hard once you put in a little practice. Everybody needs a go-to biscuit recipe, so I've included several in this chapter, along with some favorite rolls, corn breads, and even hush puppies. There's something here to round out any meal.

*Me at the weekly card game*

*Our friend, Cliff, at the card game*

# Friends & Family

FRANK AND I ARE VERY FORTUNATE to have close family and friends in our lives. When we lost our son, Frank Jr., 9 years ago, all our friends were here for us in so many ways. Our car club buddies came to our home and brought a lot of food, love, and support. Our church family at First Assembly of God in St. Paul, Virginia, and many of our other friends brought food to our house and to our daughter-in-law's house. The love and support of our friends was just so sweet, and it meant the world to me. I don't know how we would have made it through without them.

*Franki, my granddaughter, with her sons Asher and Jesse*

It's important to have friends and family who are there to encourage you during the good times, too. When I was on *Huckabee* in Nashville last year, my family came in to to town to celebrate my accomplishments and spend time together. Then, even more recently, I ran into one of my best friends in the grocery store. She hugged me, and she said she was so happy I was getting to write a cookbook. She told me it was my turn to enjoy something good and that I deserved this opportunity. It felt good to hear someone tell me that. We're also fortunate to have friends in our car club we enjoy spending time with at car shows or during weekly card games. All of these people build me up and keep me going.

*Me holding Jr. on his birthday*

I believe you should treat people the way you want to be treated. I am so blessed by a wonderful, loving family and so many good friends. God is so good to me, and He takes care of my needs.

*Frank holding Franki*

*Family at the taping for* Huckabee *in Nashville*

Weekly card game with our friends, Cliff and Barbara Hare

A vase I made with a dried gourd and flowers from Frank Jr.'s funeral

Lisa, Elizabeth, and Franki on my porch reading a book in the early 1990s

Car club picnic

Asher and Mamaw Linda sharing a laugh at the pizza place

## Mother & Father's Love

God blessed us with a baby boy
So many years ago
We watched him and loved him
And we saw him grow

We loved him so very much
Loved his beautiful smile
We held his hand in ours
For a long while

We watched him grow every day
To be gentle and kind
He touched so many people
A better friend you couldn't find

He loved the Lord
With all his heart
He tried to help others
From the very start

We held your little hands
And gave you all our love,
Now God holds your hands
In your home above

A piece of our hearts are broken
And our lives won't be the same
But God needed a special angel
And He called out your name

We know you are with God now
In His loving care
And someday, my precious son,
We will meet you up there

We love you so much

Mommy & Daddy

*(Written on the night before Frank Jr.'s funeral. I couldn't sleep, so I wrote him this poem.)*

# Zucchini Cornbread

*I like this twist on traditional cornbread. Sometime it's nice to have something with a little different flavor. I also like that it's an easy, stir-together recipes.*

*Makes 1 (9-inch) pan*

1½ cups shredded zucchini, patted dry
1¼ cups self-rising cornmeal
¾ cup cottage cheese
6 tablespoons salted butter, melted
¼ cup self-rising flour
¼ cup vegetable oil
1 small onion, finely chopped
3 large eggs, beaten
1 tablespoon white sugar

1. Preheat oven to 425°. Grease a 9-inch square baking pan.

2. In a medium bowl, mix all ingredients together, and place in prepared pan.

3. Bake for 30 to 35 minutes.

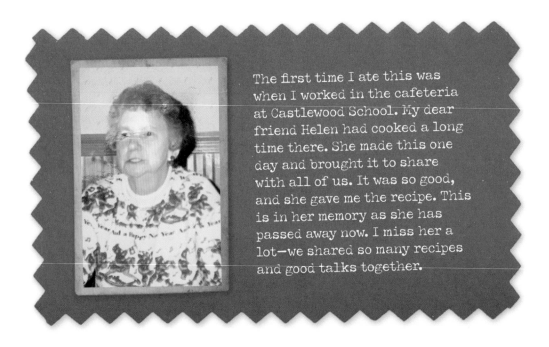

The first time I ate this was when I worked in the cafeteria at Castlewood School. My dear friend Helen had cooked a long time there. She made this one day and brought it to share with all of us. It was so good, and she gave me the recipe. This is in her memory as she has passed away now. I miss her a lot—we shared so many recipes and good talks together.

# Hush Puppies

*Frank says my Hush Puppies are the best, and I always make them when we eat catfish. They're easy and good and everyone loves them.*

*Makes 36*

**Vegetable oil, for frying**
**1½   cups cornmeal**
**½    cup all-purpose flour**
**2     tablespoons white sugar**
**2     teaspoons baking powder**
**½    teaspoon table salt**
**1     small onion, finely chopped**
**1     large egg, beaten**
**¾    cup whole buttermilk**

1. Heat oil in a Dutch oven until oil reaches 350°.

2. In a medium mixing bowl, sift together cornmeal, flour, sugar, baking powder, and salt; add onion. Blend in egg and buttermilk. Drop batter by tablespoonfuls into hot oil, frying only a few at a time. Fry until golden brown. Let drain on paper towels.

*Laundry needlepoint craft*

## Wash Day Blues

Monday morning rolls around
Time to wash clothes again
There's always plenty to do
A week it's only been

Wash and scrub them
And clean them real fine
Carry them outside
And hang them on the line

Let them dry all day
In the hot sun
Getting your clothes clean
Can keep you on a run

Most of them will need
An iron and an ironing board
Just give me strength
To get it all done, Lord

Doing laundry today
Is easier than it used to be
The job is less work
For you and me

Generations before ours used washboards to scrub dirty laundry. They would have a big tub filled with water and soap—my grandmother used Lye soap. They had to scrub the clothes on the washboard, wring them out by hand, then rinse them and wring them out again and hang them on the line to dry. My mommy and grandmother both had heavy flat irons they had to heat on the cookstove to iron their clothes. All I can say is, baby we've come a long way, and thank goodness for modern inventions.

# Pineapple Zucchini Bread

*My family and friends love this bread. I like making it into mini loaves so I can wrap them up and give them for gifts.*

*Makes 2 (9x5-inch) loaves or 6 mini loaves*

| | |
|---|---|
| 2 | cups white sugar |
| 1 | cup vegetable oil |
| 3 | large eggs |
| 2 | teaspoons vanilla extract |
| 3 | cups all-purpose flour |
| 2 | cups shredded zucchini, patted dry |
| 1 | (8-ounce) can crushed pineapple, well drained |
| 1 | cup chopped pecans |
| 2 | teaspoons baking soda |
| 1½ | teaspoons ground cinnamon |
| 1 | teaspoon table salt |
| ¾ | teaspoon ground nutmeg |
| ¼ | teaspoon baking powder |

1. Preheat oven to 350°. Grease and flour 2 (9x5-inch) loaf pans or 6 mini loaf pans.

2. In a large mixing bowl, whisk sugar, oil, eggs, and vanilla until thick. Stir in flour and all remaining ingredients. Blend well. Pour into prepared pans.

3. Bake until a toothpick inserted in middle comes out clean, about 45 to 50 minutes.

*❧ I gave a loaf of this bread to our friends, Wayne and Peggy. The next day, they brought me a whole basket of fresh zucchini. I think they were hinting for more! ❧*

*Peggy and Wayne Hamilton at a drive-in with their custom 1937 Packard*

# Cheesy-Garlic Biscuits

*I came up with this recipe a few years ago. I like the ones at buffet restaurants, so I experimented until I got them just right. I can eat them all by themselves because they're so good.*

*Makes 15*

**BISCUITS:**

2½  cups all-purpose baking mix*
¾   cup shredded mild Cheddar cheese
1   teaspoon garlic powder
1   teaspoon ranch seasoning mix*
1   cup whole buttermilk

**TOPPING:**

½   cup salted butter, melted
½   teaspoon garlic powder
½   teaspoon ranch seasoning mix*
¼   teaspoon ground black pepper

1. Preheat oven to 450°. Grease a large baking sheet.

2. For the biscuits: In a large bowl, mix together baking mix, cheese, garlic powder, and ranch mix. Stir in buttermilk just until moistened. Drop by tablespoonfuls into 15 mounds onto prepared pan.

3. Bake until golden brown, 10 to 12 minutes.

4. For the topping: In a small bowl, mix together all ingredients, and brush onto hot biscuits.

*I use Bisquick and Hidden Valley Ranch Dressing Mix

## My Greatest Blessings

The sun is shining through my window
On this beautiful day
I'm planning on enjoying it
In every way

God has blessed me in so many ways
I can't begin to count them
Even though I try hard
To give thanks every day to Him

I have a loving family
That I know I can count on for love
To help me through my sickness
And I have the Lord above

I just lost my oldest brother
He meant the world to me
But I know someday in Heaven
He again I will get to see

Life goes by way too fast
Never enough time to tell people how you feel
I have had a good and happy life
This is so real

I love all of you family
With all my soul and heart
I hope we have a lot of time together
Before we have to part

The Lord loves you all and so do I.

# Rolls

*This roll recipe is great for anyone starting out making yeast breads. It's easy and always turns out good. Frank insists on eating 2 of them with butter as soon as I take them out of the oven!*

*Makes 40 rolls*

3¾  **cups lukewarm water, divided (105°)**
3  **(.25-ounce) packages active dry yeast**
9  **cups all-purpose flour**
¾  **cup white sugar**
2  **tablespoons table salt**
1½  **teaspoons baking powder**
¾  **cup all-vegetable shortening***
3  **large eggs, beaten well**
**Melted butter, for brushing**

1. Combine ¾ cup lukewarm water and yeast in a bowl to dissolve.

2. Mix flour, sugar, salt, and baking powder together, and cut in shortening. Pour beaten eggs into flour mixture. Stir in dissolved yeast. Add remaining 3 cups lukewarm water to make a lightweight batter. Place dough into a large greased bowl; cover with dish towel, and let rise until doubled, about 1 hour.

3. Butter baking sheets.

4. Push down dough. Divide in half, and roll out to ½-inch thickness on a floured surface; cut out rolls using a 2½-inch cutter, and place on prepared pans. Repeat with remaining half of dough. Cover again, and let rise in a warm place until doubled, about 1 hour.

5. Preheat oven to 400°.

6. Bake until lightly browned, 10 to 12 minutes. Brush tops of rolls with melted butter.

*\*I use Crisco.*

# Mexican Cornbread

*This cornbread goes with just about everything! We love having it with Taco Soup (recipe page 97), chili beans, or even by itself.*

*Makes 1 (13x9-inch) pan*

**2** cups yellow self-rising cornmeal mix

**1** (8-ounce) can cream-style corn

**2** cups shredded mild Cheddar cheese, divided

**1** cup whole buttermilk

**⅔** cup vegetable oil

**1** (4-ounce) can mild green chiles

**1** small onion, chopped

**2** large eggs

**1** tablespoon white sugar

1. Preheat oven to 400°. Grease a 13x9-inch baking pan.

2. In a medium mixing bowl, mix cornmeal, corn, 1½ cups cheese, buttermilk, oil, chiles, onion, eggs, and sugar together, and pour into prepared pan. Sprinkle remaining ½ cup cheese on top of mixture.

3. Bake until lightly browned, 25 to 30 minutes.

We go to the Breaks Park Car Show every July, and our friend Shanghi usually asks me to make him a pan of Mexican Cornbread. He and his wife like it a lot, and so do a lot of our other friends and family.

# Red Chili Biscuits

*I made these a few years ago out of curiosity. I found them in an old book, and I worked up my own version that I think is really good.*

*Makes 15*

2     **cups all-purpose flour**
1     **tablespoon white sugar**
1     **tablespoon baking powder**
1     **teaspoon table salt**
⅓     **cup lard or all-vegetable shortening***
½     **cup shredded mild Cheddar cheese**
1½   **cups Sourdough Starter (recipe page 126)**
1     **tablespoon chili powder**

1. Preheat oven to 400°. Grease a large baking sheet.

2. Mix the flour up with sugar, baking powder, and salt. Cut in lard or shortening until it looks like fine meal. Toss in cheese, Sourdough Starter, and chili powder. Mix until flour is moistened. Place on a floured surface; knead lightly, and pat to ½-inch thickness. Cut with a 2½-inch cutter. Put biscuits on prepared pan.

3. Bake for 20 to 25 minutes.

*\*I use Crisco.*

*I love collecting cookbooks. These are some of my favorites I've gathered over the years.*

# Buttermilk Biscuits

*I have been making these ever since I got married at age 16.
I wasn't a very good cook at first, but as they say, practice makes
perfect. I used to fry tenderloin or sausage to put on a biscuit
for Frank to take to lunch when he worked in the coal mines.*

*Makes about 14*

| | |
|---|---|
| 2 | cups all-purpose flour |
| 1 | tablespoon baking powder |
| ½ | teaspoon table salt |
| ¼ | teaspoon baking soda |
| 6 | tablespoons cold salted butter |
| 1 | cup whole buttermilk, plus more for brushing |

**Serve with butter, Sausage Gravy, Slow Cooker Apple Butter, or Pumpkin Butter (recipes page 188)**

1. Preheat oven to 450°.

2. In a mixing bowl, mix together flour, baking powder, salt, and baking soda. Cut in butter until it looks like coarse crumbs. Stir in buttermilk and continue stirring until dough clings together and makes a ball. Knead dough 10 times on lightly floured surface. Roll into a rectangle about ½-inch thick. Cut out with a 2-inch biscuit cutter, rerolling scraps as necessary. Place 1 inch apart on a baking sheet. Brush tops with buttermilk.

3. Bake until golden brown, about 14 to 17 minutes.

*One of my favorite ways to eat these biscuits is with Slow Cooker Apple Butter (recipe page 188). When I was growing up, my mommy would make Apple Butter outside in a big pot. It always smelled so good. It's a lot easier this way!*

# Favorite Biscuit Toppings

## Sausage Gravy

*Makes about 3½ cups*

1    **(16-ounce) pork sausage roll**
¼    **cup all-purpose flour**
2    **cups whole milk**
**Table salt and ground black pepper, to taste**

1. In a large cast-iron skillet, cook pork sausage over medium heat until browned. Stir in flour, and cook, stirring constantly, for 2 minutes. Gradually stir in milk. Cook, stirring frequently, until thick and bubbly. Season with salt and pepper.

## Slow Cooker Apple Butter

*Makes about 12 cups*

12    **cups applesauce**
9    **cups white sugar**
¼    **cup white distilled vinegar**
¼    **cup lemon juice**
½    **cup cinnamon hot candy**

1. Combine all ingredients in a 6-quart slow cooker. Cover and cook about 5 to 6 hours more. Uncover and continue to cook until thickened, about 5 to 6 hours, stirring occasionally.

2. Ladle into hot jars, leaving ½-inch of headspace. Cover with lids and rings. Process for 10 minutes in a boiling water bath in canner. Let cool completely on a wire rack. Check to make sure lids are sealed.

## Pumpkin Butter

*Makes about 6 cups*

6½    **pounds pie pumpkins**
3    **cups firmly packed light brown sugar**
2    **teaspoons ground cinnamon**
1    **teaspoon table salt**
1    **teaspoon ground nutmeg**
1    **teaspoon lemon zest**
¼    **teaspoon fresh lemon juice**

1. Peel, seed, and cut up pumpkin. Place pumpkin in a large pot and add water to cover. Bring to a boil over medium-high heat; boil until pumpkin is tender, about 10 minutes. Drain and mash pumpkin. Whip with a hand mixer until smooth. (You should have 6½ cups pumpkin purée.)

2. In the same large pot, combine pumpkin purée and remaining ingredients, and bring to a boil over medium-high heat. Boil and stir constantly for 10 minutes.

3. Ladle into hot jars, leaving ½-inch of headspace. Cover with lids and rings. Process for 10 minutes in a boiling water bath in canner. Let cool completely on a wire rack. Check to make sure lids are sealed.

# CHAPTER 9

# Cakes

Cakes always feel special to me, whether they're served at a holiday party, potluck dinner, or just a regular family meal. I've included some of my favorite cake recipes in this chapter—some are simple sheet cakes and others are a little fancy. I bet you'll find at least one new recipe here you can make for your next function or family gathering.

Dump Cake is an easy weeknight dessert

Blue ribbon from Mike Huckabeee

# Sudden Fame

*Filming for* Talk of Alabama *in Birmingham, Alabama*

IF YOU HAD ASKED ME A YEAR AGO what "going viral" meant, I don't think I could have told you. No one was more surprised than I was when I became famous overnight in the summer of 2022. Yes, I had won dozens of ribbons at the Virginia-Kentucky District Fair, but to be honest, that wasn't really anything new. I'd been entering fairs since 1983 and always won ribbons (I have 1,400 total that I've been able to find and count). It was just part of my life, and most people probably hadn't thought too much about it. The fact that I was suddenly in the news—stations like NPR were doing stories on me while videos about me TikTok (I didn't even know what that was) were getting hundreds of thousands of views—was unexpected.

People ask me all the time how I feel about becoming so well-known (by accident) at the age of 74. I tell them I feel proud, and I'm happy to be able to share my love of baking, canning, and crafting with the world. I think it's helping to bring back an interest in county fair competitions for young people. One of my local fairs told me that after my story broke in June, their Home Economics competition several months later went from having its usual number of about 100 entrants to having over 300 competitors! That makes me happy to hear. And whether people are entering fairs or not, I hope they're interested in carrying on some of these traditions of the past that I was worried had been dying out.

I've gotten to do a lot of wonderful things in the last year. I've gone to New York to film for the *Today Show*, Los Angeles for *The Kelly Clarkson Show*, and Nashville for *Huckabee*. I went to Birmingham, Alabama to visit my publisher and work on my cookbook in their test kitchens. I've done many local news channel interviews and podcasts and Zoom interviews with people all over the United States and in Europe. One of my favorite stories is that one of Virginia's senators, Mark Warner, wanted to meet me and exchange recipes. I gave him my recipe for Twinkie Surprise, and he gave me his Tuna Melt recipe along with a commendation. I've gotten some local awards and was asked to come to my grandkid's school as a guest speaker to teach them how to make biscuits. Several times when I've been in the grocery store, I've been stopped and asked to take a picture with someone, like I'm a celebrity! I've even made phone calls to the pharmacy or dentist and been asked, "Are you THE Linda Skeens?". This attention has certainly all come as a shock to me, but it hasn't been unwelcomed. Everyone has been so kind.

*Signing my cookbook contract*

MARK R. WARNER
VIRGINIA

UNITED STATES SENATOR
WASHINGTON, D.C.

August 22, 2022

Dear Ms. Skeens,

I am pleased to extend my warmest congratulations to you upon winning 25 contests at the 109th Virginia-Kentucky District Fair for your baked and canned goods.

This recognition serves as a tribute to your dedication to excellence and your culinary skills. Throughout the years, you have brought joy to family and friends by sharing your baking and cooking with them. As you have entered these treats for judging at the annual fair each year, it has become clear to those in Southwest Virginia just how talented you are. Following this year's honors, the article about you in *The Washington Post*, and your appearance on the *Today Show*, individuals across the United States are now looking to you for recipe tips and anxious to sample your dishes. I commend you for your hard work and willingness to share your talent with others.

On this important occasion, I am very pleased to join with your family, friends, and community in saluting your accomplishments and wishing you success in all of your future endeavors.

Sincerely,

Mark R. Warner

MARK R. WARNER
United States Senator

*A letter I received from Senator Mark Warner*

*Getting ready to film a few segments at WJHL in Johnson City, Tennessee*

*Me and Brian Hart Hoffman in the 83 Press test kitchen in Birmingham, Alabama*

*Russell County Board of Supervisors gave me this plaque recognizing my achievements*

*The 83 Press cookbook team visiting with me at my home in Virginia*

# Ginger Ale Pound Cake

*I love a good Southern pound cake, especially one that has interesting flavors, like this one. It may take a little while to bake, but it's worth the time—so be patient.*

*Makes 1 (15-cup) Bundt cake*

1      cup salted butter
½      cup all-vegetable shortening*, plus more for greasing pan
2½    cups white sugar
5      large eggs
3      cups all-purpose flour, plus more for greasing pan
1      teaspoon baking powder
¾      cup plus 2 to 3 teaspoons ginger ale, divided
2      teaspoons vanilla extract
2      teaspoons lemon flavoring
½      teaspoon table salt
1      cup powdered sugar

1. Preheat oven to 325°. Grease a 15-cup Bundt pan with shortening and dust with flour.

2. In a large bowl, beat butter and shortening at medium speed until creamy. Mix in sugar. Add eggs, one at a time, beating well after each addition. Add flour, baking powder, and ¾ cup ginger ale. Then, add vanilla, lemon flavoring, and salt. Continue beating for 5 minutes. Pour batter into prepared pan.

3. Bake for 1½ hours or until done. Let cool completely in pan.

4. In a small bowl, mix powdered sugar and remaining 2 to 3 teaspoons ginger ale. Drizzle over cooled cake.

*I use Crisco.

My husband's cousin Bobby Skeens and his wife, Sis, gave me this recipe. Sis makes things "old school" like I do, and we like to spend time together. We pray for each other, go to Golden Corral to eat, and love to do a lot of the same things.

# Carrot Cake

*Some carrot cakes can be intimidating with lots of layers and stacking. This is a simpler version that tastes just as good! I like that it bakes in a 13x9 pan because that makes it easy to take to a picnic or potluck dinner.*

*Makes 1 (13x9-inch) cake*

**CAKE:**
| | |
|---|---|
| 2 | **cups white sugar** |
| ¾ | **cup vegetable oil** |
| ¾ | **cup whole buttermilk** |
| 3 | **large eggs** |
| 2 | **teaspoons vanilla extract** |
| 2 | **cups all-purpose flour** |
| 2 | **teaspoons baking soda** |
| 2 | **teaspoons ground cinnamon** |
| ½ | **teaspoon table salt** |
| 1 | **(8-ounce) can crushed pineapples, drained** |
| 2 | **cups grated carrots** |
| 1 | **cup flaked sweetened coconut** |
| 1 | **cup chopped pecans** |
| ½ | **cup raisins** |

**Cream Cheese Frosting (recipe follows)**

1. Preheat oven to 350°. Grease and flour a 13x9-inch baking dish.

2. Combine sugar, oil, buttermilk, eggs, and vanilla in a bowl. Mix well.

3. In a separate bowl, combine flour, baking soda, cinnamon, and salt. Add to sugar mixture, and stir until combined.

4. Stir pineapple, carrots, coconut, pecans, and raisins into the batter, and pour into prepared pan.

5. Bake for 45 to 50 minutes. Let cool completely in pan. Spread Cream Cheese Frosting on cooled cake.

**CREAM CHEESE FROSTING:**

*Makes 2 ½ cups*
| | |
|---|---|
| ½ | **cup salted butter, softened** |
| 1 | **(8-ounce) package cream cheese, softened** |
| 1 | **(16-ounce) box powdered sugar** |
| 2 | **teaspoons heavy whipping cream** |
| 1 | **teaspoon vanilla extract** |

1. Beat butter and cream cheese on medium-high speed until smooth. Add powdered sugar, cream, and vanilla. Beat on medium speed until light and fluffy. Spread onto cooled cake.

# Banana Pudding Poke Cake

*My good friend, Barb, gave me this recipe. If you like bananas, you'll love this cake. It's a twist on an old homestyle banana pudding.*

*Makes 1 (13x9-inch) cake*

1    (15.25-ounce) box yellow
     cake mix
2    (3.4-ounce) boxes banana
     instant pudding
4    cups whole milk
Sliced bananas (use your judgment)
1    (8-ounce) container frozen
     whipped topping•, thawed
20   vanilla wafers, crushed

1. Grease and flour a 13x9-inch baking dish. Bake cake in prepared dish according to package directions. Let cool for a few minutes and then poke holes all over the cake—don't be shy. Hit the bottom of the pan.

2. Next, prepare pudding by mixing the pudding mix and milk. Pour over cake before it starts to get thick. Spread evenly, filling over all holes. Refrigerate for 2 hours or until set.

3. Top with sliced bananas, whipped topping, and crushed wafers.

*\*I use Cool Whip.*

# Sugarless Spice Cake

*I like this recipe because it's good for anyone who is diabetic
or watching their sugar, and it still tastes really great!*

*Makes 1 (8-inch) cake*

| | |
|---|---|
| 2 | **cups raisins** |
| 2 | **cups water** |
| 1 | **cup unsweetened applesauce** |
| ¾ | **cup vegetable oil** |
| 2 | **large eggs, beaten** |
| 2 | **tablespoons liquid artificial sweetener** |
| 2 | **cups all-purpose flour** |
| 1 | **teaspoon baking soda** |
| 1½ | **teaspoons ground cinnamon** |
| 1 | **teaspoon vanilla extract** |
| ½ | **teaspoon ground nutmeg** |

1. Preheat oven to 350°. Grease an 8-inch square baking pan.

2. In a saucepan, add raisins and water, cook until water evaporates. Add applesauce, oil, eggs, and sweetener. Mix well. Blend in flour and baking soda. Stir in cinnamon, vanilla, and nutmeg. Pour into prepared pan.

3. Bake for 25 minutes.

## A Wish

I had a special wish
My brother I wanted to see
It's been three years since
He had got to visit me.

Growing up and still we are very close
Even though he lives far away
I think about him often
And pray for him each day.

There were seven kids in my family
All are gone but us two
We miss our brothers and sister
So very much, we really do.

His family brought him to see me
And we had a wonderful visit that day
It meant the world to me
In a special way.

I hated for the day to end.
But I'm thankful we got to see each other
You mean the world to me
My sweet baby brother.

You and I both have health problems
And sometimes life is hard for us to bear
But I know dear brother
We are both in God's care.

I love you Sammy.

# Jam Cake
## with Caramel Glaze

*My mommy used to make this one, and it was so good. She baked the cake on an old coal cookstove. She cooked the caramel glaze in an iron skillet on top of the stove. I asked her how she knew when the oven was hot enough, and she said she just knew.*

*Makes 1 (8-inch) cake*

| | |
|---|---|
| ½ | cup salted butter, softened |
| 1 | cup white sugar |
| 3 | large eggs |
| ½ | teaspoon vanilla extract |
| 1¾ | cups all-purpose flour |
| ½ | teaspoon baking soda |
| ½ | teaspoon ground allspice |
| ½ | teaspoon ground cinnamon |
| ½ | teaspoon ground cloves |
| ¼ | teaspoon table salt |
| 1 | cup Blackberry Jam (recipe page 21) |
| ½ | cup whole buttermilk |
| ½ | cup strawberry preserves |
| ½ | cup raisins |
| ½ | cup chopped black walnuts |

Caramel Glaze (recipe follows)

1. Preheat oven to 325°. Grease bottoms of 2 (8-inch) round cake pans. Line bottom of pans with parchment paper. Grease and flour paper and sides of pan.

2. In a medium bowl, beat butter and sugar with a hand mixer until light and fluffy. Add eggs, one at a time, beating well after each addition. Blend in vanilla.

3. In a small bowl, sift together flour, baking soda, allspice, cinnamon, cloves, and salt. Add flour mixture, jam, buttermilk, and preserves to butter mixture. Beat for 2 minutes at medium speed. Stir in raisins and walnuts. Pour into prepared pans.

4. Bake until toothpick inserted in centers comes out clean, 45 to 50 minutes. Let cool in pans for 10 minutes. Turn out onto wire racks. Remove paper and let cool completely.

5. Place one cake layer on serving plate. Cover with ⅓ cup warm Caramel Glaze. Top with second cake layer, and drizzle with remaining Caramel Glaze.

*This cake is best made 2 days in advance. Store tightly covered. Don't refrigerate. You can bake in a greased and floured 13x9-inch pan, too.*

### CARAMEL GLAZE:
*Makes 2½ cups*

| | |
|---|---|
| ¼ | cup salted butter |
| ½ | cup firmly packed dark brown sugar |
| ¼ | cup whole milk |
| 2 | cups powdered sugar |
| 1 | teaspoon vanilla extract |

1. Melt butter in a saucepan over medium-low heat. Stir in brown sugar; cook, stirring constantly, for 2 minutes. Add milk, and continue cooking until mixture boils, stirring constantly. Remove from heat; gradually stir in powdered sugar. Add vanilla; blend well. Use immediately.

# Coconut Cake

*This was a favorite of my daddy's. I made it for him on his birthday every year, and everyone else who eats it loves it, too. Coconut is one of my favorite ingredients to bake with.*

*Makes 1 (13x9-inch) cake*

1    (15.25-oz) package yellow cake mix
1    (7-ounce) bag sweetened flaked coconut, divided
1¼   cups whole milk, divided
1    (3.4-ounce) package coconut instant pudding mix
1    (3.4-ounce) package vanilla instant pudding mix
¼    cup powdered sugar
1    (8-ounce) container frozen whipped topping*

1. Heat oven to 350°. Grease a 13x9-inch baking dish or pan.

2. Prepare cake mix as directed on box, and stir in ⅔ cup coconut, ¼ cup milk, and coconut pudding mix. Pour in pan and bake as directed on box for a 13x9-inch pan. Let cool completely.

3. In a large bowl, whisk vanilla pudding mix, powdered sugar, and remaining 1 cup milk for 2 minutes. Fold in whipped topping. Spread frosting on top of cake, and sprinkle remaining coconut on top of icing. Keep in fridge until ready to serve.

*I use Cool Whip for this recipe.*

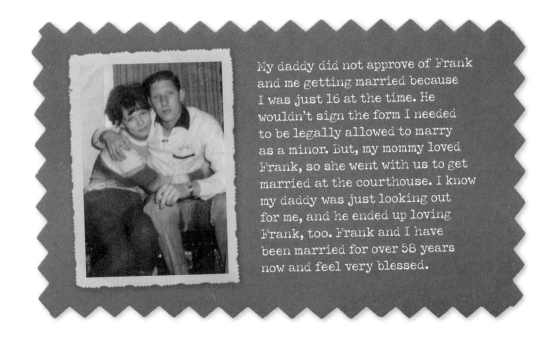

My daddy did not approve of Frank and me getting married because I was just 16 at the time. He wouldn't sign the form I needed to be legally allowed to marry as a minor. But, my mommy loved Frank, so she went with us to get married at the courthouse. I know my daddy was just looking out for me, and he ended up loving Frank, too. Frank and I have been married for over 58 years now and feel very blessed.

# Oatmeal Cake

*This cake recipe is a twist on traditional oatmeal cookies.
If you have family members who love oatmeal cookies, try making
this recipe for them—it just might be a new favorite!*

*Makes 1 (13x9-inch) cake*

1¼  cups boiling water
1  cup old-fashioned oats
½  cup unsalted butter, softened
1  cup white sugar
1  cup firmly packed light brown sugar
2  large eggs
1  teaspoon vanilla extract
1⅔  cups all-purpose flour
1  teaspoon baking soda
1  teaspoon ground cinnamon
½  teaspoon table salt
Topping (recipe follows)

1. Preheat oven to 350°. Grease and flour a 13x9-inch cake pan.

2. Pour 1¼ cups boiling water over oats in a bowl. Let stand for 20 minutes.

3. In a medium bowl, beat butter and sugar with a hand mixer until light and fluffy. Add oats, and mix well. Add eggs and vanilla, and mix until combined.

4. In a small bowl, sift together flour, baking soda, cinnamon, and salt. Add to oat mixture, and mix well. Pour into prepared pan.

5. Bake until browned, 30 to 35 minutes. Preheat broiler. Spread Topping evenly over warm cake, and place cake under broiler 2 inches from heat. Broil until lightly browned, 1 to 1½ minutes. Let cool and eat.

## TOPPING:

*Makes 2½ cups*

1  cup packed light brown sugar
1  cup unsweetened flaked coconut
¼  cup salted butter, softened
¼  cup heavy whipping cream

1. In a small bowl, mix all ingredients together until combined.

# Dump Cake

*One reason I love this Dump Cake is because it's easy—you just dump everything in a dish and bake it! I also like that it has a sweet and tart flavor combination. My sister-in-law, Jane, made it for Thanksgiving dinner one year, and I was hooked.*

*Makes 1 (13x9-inch) cake*

2    **(8-ounce) cans unsweetened crushed pineapple, undrained**
1    **(20-ounce) can cherry pie filling**
1    **(15.25-ounce) package yellow cake mix**
1    **cup water**
¼    **cup vegetable oil**
¼    **cup chopped pecans**
**Vanilla ice cream, to serve**

1. Preheat oven to 350°. Grease a 13x9-inch baking dish.

2. Spread pineapple evenly into prepared pan. Spread cherry pie filling over pineapple.

3. In a mixing bowl, stir together cake mix, water, and oil just until blended. Batter with be lumpy. Pour this over cherry pie filling. Sprinkle with pecans.

4. Bake until cake is golden brown, 40 to 45 minutes. Serve with ice cream.

## A Child in the Kitchen

If you let a child help you cook
You will probably have a mess,
How the food will turn out,
You can only guess.

You can see a face that beams
From helping you measure, stir and bake,
They will always remember
What you helped them to make.

# Pumpkin Sheet Cake
## with Cream Cheese Icing

*Anything with pumpkin always makes me think of fall. This cake is real good for Thanksgiving dinner or a fall potluck supper.*

*Makes 1 (13x9-inch) cake*

### CAKE:
| | |
|---|---|
| 1 | cup salted butter, softened |
| 2 | cups white sugar |
| 2 | cups canned pumpkin |
| ¾ | cup boiling water |
| 2 | large eggs |
| 2 | teaspoons vanilla extract |
| ½ | teaspoon maple extract |
| 2 | cups all-purpose flour |
| 2 | teaspoons baking soda |
| 2 | teaspoons pumpkin pie spice |
| ¼ | teaspoon table salt |
| ½ | cup whole buttermilk |

**Cream Cheese Icing (recipe follows)**

1. Preheat oven to 350°. Grease a 13x9-inch cake pan.

2. In a large bowl, mix butter, sugar, pumpkin, ¾ cup boiling water, eggs, and extracts until well mixed.

3. In another bowl, mix flour, baking soda, pie spice, and salt together. Add flour mixture to butter mixture alternately with buttermilk, beating well after each addition. Pour into prepared pan.

4. Bake until a toothpick inserted in center comes out clean, 25 to 30 minutes. Let cool completely. Spread Cream Cheese Icing on cooled cake.

### CREAM CHEESE ICING:

*Makes 2½ cups*

| | |
|---|---|
| 1 | (8-ounce) package cream cheese, softened |
| ½ | cup salted butter, softened |
| 1 | tablespoon whole milk |
| 1 | pound powdered sugar |

**Dash of table salt**

1. Beat cream cheese, butter, and milk with a hand mixer until well combined. Beat in powdered sugar and salt until well combined.

# Hornet's Nest Cake

*This cake is good enough on its own—no icing needed. It was my son-in-law's favorite. We miss him a lot and wish he was still here with us.*

*Makes 1 (13x9-inch) cake*

1   **(3.5-ounce) box butterscotch cook and serve pudding (not instant)**
1   **(15.5-ounce) box yellow cake mix***
1   **(12-ounce) package butterscotch chips**
1   **cup chopped pecans**

1. Preheat oven to 350°. Grease a 13x9-inch cake pan.

2. In a large saucepan, prepare pudding according to directions on box. Add dry cake mix. Mix just until moistened. Pour into prepared pan. Sprinkle butterscotch chips and nuts on top.

3. Bake until a wooden pick inserted into cake comes out clean, 25 to 30 minutes.

*\*I use Betty Crocker Super Moist Butter Yellow Cake Mix.*

**Blue Ribbon Tip**
Substitute chocolate cake mix, chocolate pudding, and chocolate chips for a different flavor.

# Molasses Cake

*This old-fashioned cake is made with spices and flavors that are just right for Christmastime. Baking it will make your whole house smell good.*

*Makes 1 (9-inch) cake*

½ cup salted butter, softened
1 cup firmly packed light brown sugar
3 large eggs
1 cup molasses
3 cups self-rising flour
1 tablespoon ground ginger
1 teaspoon ground cinnamon
½ teaspoon ground allspice
1 cup whole buttermilk
1½ cups apple butter
**Garnish: powdered sugar**

1. Preheat oven to 350°. Grease 4 (9-inch) round cake pans.

2. With a hand mixer, beat butter and brown sugar together. Beat in eggs and molasses.

3. Mix flour, ginger, cinnamon, and allspice. Add flour mixture to butter mixture alternately with buttermilk, beating until combined after each addition. Pour evenly into prepared pans.

4. Bake for about 10 minutes or until done. Spread ½ cup apple butter between each layer and stack. Garnish with powdered sugar, if desired

*Blue Ribbon Tip*
You can use my recipe for Slow Cooker Apple Butter (recipe page 188) between each layer, but if you don't have time to make it, store-bought works fine, too.

# CHAPTER 10

## Cookies & Pies

The recipes in this chapter are some of my favorite baked goods to make for fair competitions and bake sales. I made many of these more times than I can count, and I still enjoy them every time I make them. If it's a really good recipe, you never grow tired of it. I hope you all enjoy these cookies and pies as much as my family and I do.

*Giving Lucy Peanut Butter Balls*

*My Oatmeal Cookies have won lots of ribbons*

# Beloved Pets

*Me and Milo, a stray I took in*

ANIMALS HAVE ALWAYS HAD a special place in my life and my heart. We've had all kinds of pets. Grunt, my last dog, was more like my kid. He was with me always. When we lost our son, Frank Jr., I would cry, and Grunt would try to comfort me and make me feel better. He just knew that something was bothering me. We lost Grunt 8 years ago, and it broke my heart. Now we have a granddog, Lucy, who belongs to Cathy. Frank babysits Lucy when Cathy and I go shopping, and he always enjoys it. All the cats and dogs we've ever owned have been rescue animals, and I loved each and every one. Animals don't ask a lot from you—just your love. I like to make Peanut Butter Dog Treats and Peanut Butter Balls for the dogs in our family every Christmas. They also make wonderful gifts to give to other dog lovers to share with their fur babies.

*Cathy holding Lucy*

*Grunt was my buddy*

*Rollie was another special fur baby*

## Lucy

Lucy is a little dog
The apple of her mommy's eye
She's cute as a button
And sweeter than cherry pie

She has lots of toys
To play with every day
But she loves to take a nap
More than she likes to play

Lucy has lots of cats in her home
Eleven at last count of them
They are very playful on their cat tree
They go from limb to limb

One of the cats loves to
Chase and pull Lucy's tail,
It makes her nervous
And she will let out a yell

She loves to come to Mamaw's house
While Mommy goes out shopping,
She keeps her Mamaw busy
On her toes and hopping

She is a very happy dog
When her Mommy comes back,
She usually brings a toy
In her grocery sack

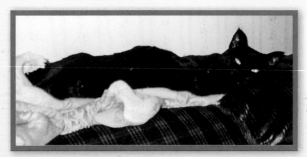

*We found Bandit at a car wash. She was so small she had to be bottle fed. She lived to be 17 years old.*

# Peanut Butter Dog Treats

*Makes about 12 (3-inch) dog treats*

**2  cups whole wheat flour**
**2  large eggs**
**½  cup creamy peanut butter**
**¼  cup water**

1. Preheat oven to 350°.

2. Mix together flour, eggs, and peanut butter in a bowl. Slowly stir in ¼ cup water; roll out to ½-inch thickness on a floured surface. Cut out with a dog bone cookie cutter, rerolling scraps as necessary. Put on wax paper-lined cookie sheets, and bake for 15 minutes. Let cool completely.

# Peanut Butter Balls

*Makes about 12*

**2  cups old-fashioned oats, divided**
**½  cup creamy peanut butter**
**¼  cup canned pumpkin purée**

1. Set aside ½ cup of the oats.

2. Stir together peanut butter, pumpkin pureé, and remaining oats until combined. Roll into small balls and place on wax paper-lined cookie sheet. Put in fridge for 30 minutes to set.

3. Put remaining 1½ cups oats on a plate. Roll balls in oatmeal until coated.

# Oatmeal Cookies

*This is probably my favorite cookie. My mommy loved them, too.
I think some of the unexpected ingredients, like dried cherries
and macadamia nuts, makes these feel special.*

*Makes about 36*

1    **cup salted butter, softened**
1    **cup firmly packed light brown sugar**
½    **cup white sugar**
2    **eggs, room temperature**
1    **tablespoon honey**
2    **teaspoons vanilla extract**
2½    **cups quick-cook oats**
1½    **cups all-purpose flour**
1    **teaspoon baking soda**
½    **teaspoon table salt**
½    **teaspoon ground cinnamon**
1¼    **cups dried cherries**
1    **cup white chocolate chips**
½    **cup chopped macadamia nuts**

1. Preheat oven to 350°. Line a large cookie sheet with parchment paper.

2. In a large bowl, cream butter and sugars with hand mixer at medium speed, until light and fluffy, about 3 minutes, stopping occasionally to scrape down bowl. Beat in eggs, honey, and vanilla.

3. In a medium bowl, combine oats, flour, baking soda, salt, and cinnamon.

Gradually beat dry ingredients into butter mixture. Fold in cherries, chocolate chips, and macadamia nuts.

4. Scoop heaping tablespoon of dough, and place dough at least 2 inches apart on prepared cookie sheet.

5. Bake until golden brown, 10 to 15 minutes. Allow to cool on the cookie sheet for 2 minutes. Place on wire racks; let cool completely.

*Me and my brothers
Carl and Sammy*

# Peach Hand Pies

*These are good for taking to bake sales or potlucks because they're easy to pack into a basket and are great hand-held treats.*

*Makes 24*

1    (8-ounce) package cream cheese, softened
1    cup unsalted butter, softened
2    cups all-purpose flour, plus more for dusting
¾    teaspoon table salt
1    (21-ounce) can peach pie filling, chopped
1    egg yolk
2    tablespoons water
**Garnish: white sugar**

1. In a medium bowl, beat cream cheese and butter with a hand mixer at medium speed until smooth.

2. In a small bowl, mix together flour and salt. Gradually, add the flour mixture to the butter mixture, and mix until dough comes together. Divide dough in half. Shape each half into a ball. Using the palm of your hand, gently flatten both pieces of dough into the shape of a disk. Wrap each disk in a plastic wrap and chill for 1 hour.

3. Preheat oven to 425°.

4. On a lightly floured surface, divide each portion of dough into 12 balls. Roll each ball into a 4-inch circle. Place one tablespoon peach pie filling on one side of each circle.

5. In a small bowl, whisk egg yolk and 2 tablespoons water together. Brush edges of pies with egg wash. Fold pastry over filling, and seal edges with a fork.

6. Place pies 2 inches apart on ungreased baking sheets. Brush tops of pie dough with remaining egg wash, and sprinkle with sugar. Cut a slit in each pie.

7. Bake until golden brown, 12 minutes. Garnish with sugar, if desired.

**Blue Ribbon Tip**
You can use canned Pillsbury Grand Biscuits in place of making the pie dough yourself to save time.

# Chocolate Chip Cookies

*These have won a lot of ribbons, but more importantly, they're a favorite of my grandkids. It's always good to have a foolproof Chocolate Chip Cookie recipe in your back pocket.*

*Makes about 36*

| | |
|---|---|
| ¾ | cup unsalted butter, softened |
| ¾ | cup firmly packed light brown sugar |
| ½ | cup white sugar |
| 2 | large eggs |
| 2 | teaspoons vanilla extract |
| 2 | cups all-purpose flour |
| 1½ | teaspoons table salt |
| 1 | teaspoon baking soda |
| 1 | (12-ounce) package semisweet chocolate chips |

1. Preheat oven to 375°. Grease a large cookie sheet.

2. Cream butter and sugars together in a bowl until light and fluffy. Add eggs and vanilla; beat well. Mix flour, salt, and baking soda. Blend into creamed mixture. Stir in chocolate chips. Drop by level tablespoonfuls 2 inches apart on prepared cookie sheet.

3. Bake 10 to 12 minutes. Let cool completely on wire racks.

## Grandchildren

Grandchildren are like flowers
That bloom in the spring
They can lift you up
And much happiness they can bring

When you talk on the phone
And let them sing to you
And see pictures of them
In all that they do

To sit and color a picture with them
Or watch a TV show
Every time you see them
How fast they do grow

At Christmas time opening their gifts
Wrapping and bows tossed all around
Hear them yell with delight
Such a happy sound

When we blow bubbles outside
Or use colorful chalk
They draw beautiful pictures
On the sidewalk

To see them build a snowman
And have so much fun
It brings lots of joy
To each and every one

*My grandbabies mean more to me than anything, and I cherish all the good memories I have made with them. I love being their Mamaw.*

# Nutty Buddy Pie

*A friend shared this recipe with me years ago. I love that the recipe makes 3 pies. I like to get one out to serve when I first make it and keep the other 2 in the freezer until we have a church function to go to or invite friends over for dinner.*

*Makes 3 (9-inch) pies*

1    (8-ounce) package cream cheese, softened
1    cup whole milk
2    cups powdered sugar
⅔    cup crunchy peanut butter
1    (16-ounce) container frozen whipped topping,* thawed
3    (6-ounce) packages graham cracker piecrust
**Chocolate syrup and roasted salted peanuts, for topping**

1. In a large bowl, whisk together cream cheese, milk, sugar, peanut butter, and whipped topping. Divide evenly among the piecrusts. Drizzle with chocolate syrup, and sprinkle with crushed peanuts. Freeze until firm, at least 3 hours. Let stand 10 minutes before serving.

*I use Cool Whip for this recipe.*

**Blue Ribbon Tip**
Allow your pie to set fully before wrapping tightly in plastic wrap. Now, it's good to keep in your freezer for a few months!

# Frozen Strawberry Pie

*I love this one, especially when fresh strawberries are in season. This pie is good to make a few days ahead when you know you'll have company coming into town because it can stay frozen until you're ready for it.*

*Makes 2 (9-inch) pies*

1   (8-ounce) package cream cheese, softened
1   cup white sugar
1½  teaspoons vanilla extract
4   cups chopped fresh strawberries
1   (8-ounce) container frozen whipped topping,* thawed
2   (9-inch) package graham cracker piecrusts

1. In a large bowl, beat together cream cheese, sugar, and vanilla with a rubber spatula until smooth. Stir in strawberries, and gently fold in whipped topping.

2. Divide filling evenly between the graham cracker piecrusts, loosely cover and freeze until firm, about 3 to 4 hours. Remove from freezer 15 minutes before serving.

*I use Cool Whip for this recipe.

**Blue Ribbon Tip**

Try switching up some ingredients for variety. You can substitute peaches or blueberries for the strawberries, and I sometimes use chocolate piecrusts instead of graham cracker crusts. Make it your own!

# No-Bake Peanut Butter Cookies

*I'm always a fan of peanut butter—I even like to eat it right off the spoon!
So, putting peanut butter into no-bake cookies is a perfect recipe for me.
If you like peanut butter, you'll love this cookie, too.*

*Makes about 69*

| | |
|---|---|
| 5 | **cups quick-cook oats** |
| 2 | **cups creamy peanut butter** |
| 1 | **cup raisins** |
| ½ | **cup sweetened flaked coconut** |
| 2 | **teaspoons vanilla extract** |
| 1 | **cup salted butter** |
| 4 | **cups white sugar** |
| 4 | **teaspoons unsweetened cocoa powder** |
| 1 | **cup whole milk** |

1. In a large bowl, mix together oats, peanut butter, raisins, coconut, and vanilla.

2. In a medium saucepan, add butter, sugar, cocoa, and milk, cook over medium heat. Allow the mixture to come to a boil for 1 minute. Remove from heat, and stir in oat mixture until combined.

3. Quickly drop cookies by heaping tablespoonfuls on wax paper, and let cool completely before serving.

# No-Bake Butterscotch Cookies

*I've always liked making these for bake sales because they're easy to make, but be aware—they go quickly! You'll probably need to make several batches to be safe.*

*Makes about 36*

| | |
|---|---|
| 2 | **cups white sugar** |
| ½ | **cup unsalted butter** |
| ⅔ | **cup evaporated milk** |
| 1 | **(3.4-ounce) package butterscotch instant pudding** |
| 3½ | **cups quick-cook oats** |
| ½ | **cup sweetened flaked coconut** |

1. In a saucepan bring sugar, butter, and evaporated milk to a boil over medium heat; Boil for 1 minute. Remove from heat and stir in pudding.

2. In a small bowl, mix together oats and coconut. Drop by level teaspoons onto waxed paper, and let cool completely before serving.

# CHAPTER 11

# Fudges & Treats

🫕 *I may be best known for some of the recipes in this chapter. I enjoy making fudges and treats for loved ones and for county fair competitions. Many of these desserts are also special to my family around the holidays. We love making memories together.*

*My prize-winning Peanut Butter Fudge*

*A favorite Christmas craft*

# Christmas Traditions

Cathy, Jr., and me

THE CHRISTMAS SEASON IS ONE OF MY favorite times of year. I love decorating my home and putting out my crafts. On Christmas Eve, the whole family comes to my house. I cook all week to get ready for them—I want to have everyone's favorite dishes. We have a meal together, open gifts, and share memories from the past year. It's a wonderful time.

Growing up, Christmas was a little different than it is now because we didn't have as much, but it was still so special. My mommy made candies and pies, and she would cook a good dinner for the family. My daddy would always go cut down a tree that us kids could decorate. There were seven kids, and I know some years must have been hard for my parents. They always made sure we each got at least one present.

If it was a good year and there was more money to go around, we would each get two presents. Back in those days, the Clinchfield Coal Company owned everything in our town of Dante, Virginia, and the surrounding areas. They owned most of the land, the stores, all the buildings—that's why so many of these kinds of towns didn't fare well after the coal companies packed up and left. But I remember the times back before that happened. The company would get Santa to come and give out little red bags with fruit and candy to all the kids in town. Kids didn't normally get things like chewing gum and store-bought candies, so it was a real treat for us.

One of my favorite traditions is the Santa Train that runs from Kentucky to Virginia and then goes on to Tennessee, stopping in different towns along the way. At each of the stops, Santa gives out toys, clothes, and food and waves at the children. I remember getting to go and see it as a little girl in Trammell, Virginia. Then, we took my kids when they were growing up, and now we take the grandkids and great-grandkids! Sometimes there are even celebrities on the train with Santa— one year they had Marty Stuart. This last year was the 80th anniversary of the train festivities here in the Appalachian Mountains.

Another thing I always enjoy doing is making Applesauce Ornaments with my grandkids. They're so much fun and keep for years! I also love making Holiday Spice Potpourri to put in my home and give as gifts to friends—it smells so good! You can make these ideas part of your own Christmas traditions.

A tree skirt I entered in the fair

Me, Frank, Lisa, and Jr. at a Christmas church social

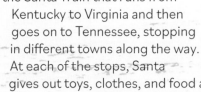

# Holiday Spice Potpourri

4  fresh oranges
4  fresh lemons
½  cup whole cloves
½  cup ground allspice
10  cinnamon sticks, broken
10  bay leaves, crumbled
4  (8-ounce) jars with lids

1. Preheat oven to 175°.

2. Using a vegetable peeler, peel oranges and lemons removing only the peel. Cut or tear into 1-inch pieces. Spread on a paper towel-lined pan. Bake for 1½ hours. Toss peels on clean paper towels, and let air dry for 24 hours. Combine dried peels with remaining ingredients. Fill jars with mixture and screw on lids.

# Applesauce Ornaments

1  pound sweetened applesauce
8  ounces ground cinnamon

1. Drain applesauce overnight. In a mixing bowl, alternate applesauce and cinnamon until mixture is consistency of cookie dough.

2. Line a rimmed baking pan with wax paper, set aside.

3. Line counter with wax paper. Take 1 cup of mixture and flatten on surface. Using decorative cookie cutters, cut out desired shapes. Place cut-out ornaments on lined pan. Using a toothpick, puncture a hole in the top of each ornament. Repeat until all dough is used.

4. Dry ornaments in a warm place for at least a day. Turn every day.

5. Once dry, string with ribbon for ornaments. For garland, string with dry fruit slices, bay leaves, and cinnamon sticks.

# Candy Bar Fudge

*This is my daughter Cathy's favorite fudge. I made some recently for a bake sale in Bristol, Virginia, and it completely sold out.*

*Makes 1 (9-inch) pan*

¾　cup salted butter
3　cups white sugar
1　(5-ounce) can evaporated milk
2　cups semi-sweet chocolate chips
1　(7-ounce) jar marshmallow creme
1　teaspoon vanilla extract
6　(2.07-ounce) candy bars*, cut into ½-inch pieces

1. Grease a foil-lined 9x9-inch square pan.

2. In a heavy saucepan, bring butter, sugar, and evaporated milk to a boil over medium heat. Cook and stir until a candy thermometer reads 234° (soft ball stage), about 3 minutes.

3. Remove from heat, stir in chocolate chips, marshmallow creme, and vanilla until smooth. Pour half the mixture in prepared pan, scatter half of candy bar pieces, and top with remaining chocolate mixture, spreading evenly. Top with remaining chopped candy bars, and let stand at room temperature until completely cool. Lift out of pan and remove foil. Cut into squares.

*I use Snickers candy bars, but other chocolate bars can also work depending on what you like.*

*Barn near Castlewood, Virginia, with a Christmas wreath*

## Blue Ribbon Tip

If you don't have a candy thermometer, look for the soft ball stage. Put cold water in a bowl, then drop just a little of the sugar mixture in the water and roll it around. If it forms a soft ball, it's ready!

# Peanut Butter Fudge

*This has become one of my most-requested desserts, both in person and on the internet! Many of my followers on social media have made it for their families and friends. If you haven't made it yet, give it a try. I hope you love it, too!*

*Makes 1 (13x9-inch) pan*

8     **tablespoons salted butter**
1     **(12-ounce) can evaporated milk**
4     **cups white sugar**
1     **cup firmly packed light brown sugar**
1     **(7-ounce) jar marshmallow creme**
1     **teaspoon vanilla extract**
1     **(16-ounce) jar creamy peanut butter**

1. Grease and line with foil a 13x9-inch pan.

2. In a large saucepan, bring butter, evaporated milk, and sugars to a boil, stirring frequently; boil for 7 minutes, continuously stirring.

3. Remove pan from heat, and stir in marshmallow creme, vanilla, and peanut butter. Pour fudge into prepared pan. Refrigerate until firm, about 4 hours. Cut in squares.

Our son's best friend, Jerry Couch, shared this recipe with me, and I've won blue ribbons with it. Thank you, Jerry, for the recipe—but most of all, thank you for being the wonderful friend to our son that you were. God bless you, always.

### For my son, Frank, Jr.

*(Words I imagine he might say to me. He is deeply loved and missed.)*

I didn't mean to cause you pain
My time had simply come,
All the work that I was meant to do
On this Earth had been done.

I'm safely home in Heaven now
Where eternal peace is mine,
and where, when God has called you, too
I will be forever thine.

# Piña Colada Fudge

*This one I found about 10 years ago in an old cookbook I bought at a yard sale.*
*I fixed up the recipe, and it's now my daughter Elizabeth's favorite.*

*Makes 1 (8x8-inch) pan*

½ **cup sweetened flaked coconut**
1 **(3.25-ounce) jar macadamia nuts, chopped**
2 **cups white chocolate chips**
1 **(16-ounce) can creamy vanilla cake icing***
½ **cup chopped dried pineapple**
1 **teaspoon rum flavoring**
1 **teaspoon coconut flavoring**

1. Preheat oven to 350°. Line an 8x8-inch pan with foil, letting excess extend over sides of pan.

2  Spread coconut and macadamia nuts on 2 separate rimmed baking sheets or small baking pans. Bake, stirring occasionally until light golden brown, 5-8 minutes. Reserve ¼ cup macadamia nuts to top fudge.

3. In a medium microwave-safe bowl, add chocolate chips. Microwave on medium for 1½ to 2 minutes or until melted, stirring in 15 second intervals until smooth. Stir in coconut, macadamia nuts, vanilla icing, pineapple, rum flavoring, coconut flavoring. Spread into prepared pan, and sprinkle with reserved ¼ cup nuts. Refrigerate for 1 hour or until firm. Lift foil edges and remove fudge from pan. Cut into squares.

*I use Pillsbury Vanilla Icing.*

*A holiday sweatshirt I made and entered in the fair*

*A snowman craft I made from a paint roller*

# Creamsicle Fudge

*This fudge tastes like ice cream in the summertime, but my family loves eating it at Christmas. It's real pretty, so it always sells well at bake sales.*

*Makes 1 (13x9-inch) pan*

¾  cup salted butter
3  cups white sugar
1  (5-ounce) can evaporated milk
1  (12-ounce) package white chocolate chips
1  (7-ounce) jar marshmallow creme
1  tablespoon orange extract
6  drops yellow food coloring
3  drops red food coloring

1. Grease a 13x9-inch pan.

2. In a large saucepan, bring butter, sugar, and evaporated milk to a boil over medium heat. Stir constantly for 5 minutes. Remove from heat, and stir in chocolate chips, marshmallow creme, and orange extract. Reserve 1 cup fudge mixture. Pour the remaining fudge in prepared pan.

3. In a small bowl, add reserved fudge mixture. Add yellow food coloring, and stir. Stir in red food coloring one drop at a time until orange color is achieved. Dollop over fudge batter, and swirl with a knife. Chill in fridge until set, about 4 hours. Cut into squares.

### Christmas Time

Christmas is coming soon
Family is gathered around
Lots of good food and presents
Love and happiness abound.

If you have a family to be with
And good food to eat
And a home to live in
And shoes on your feet

Be thankful for all you have
And make the most of each day
Show someone you care for them
In a special way.

Remember Jesus is the reason
To celebrate each year
Give thanks, He loved us and
Paid a price so dear.

Sing some Christmas songs
And enjoy the time together
It might be cold and snowing
To me it's beautiful weather.

Take the time to count your blessings
Name them one by one
And it will lift your spirits
When all is said and done.

Merry Christmas to All

# Peanut Brittle

*Frank has always loved peanuts. When my cookbook team first came to visit, they brought us some Alabama peanuts. Frank cracked the bag open as soon as he could! This Peanut Brittle is one of his favorite treats.*

*Makes about 10 servings*

1    cup white sugar
1    cup dry roasted salted peanuts
½    cup light corn syrup
1    tablespoon salted butter
1    teaspoon vanilla extract
1    teaspoon baking soda

1. Line a small baking sheet with foil; grease foil.

2. In a large microwave-safe bowl, stir together sugar, peanuts, and corn syrup. Microwave on high for about 5 minutes or until bubbling, fragrant, and just starting to turn a golden mixture (about 270°). Carefully remove bowl. Stir in butter and vanilla. Microwave about 2 minutes more or until light golden brown (about 300°). Stir in baking soda.

3. Pour onto prepared pan and gently move pan back and forth to spread brittle. Let cool completely. Break into pieces. Store in an airtight container up to 3 weeks.

I've been making this classic recipe for a long time, but one time not too long ago, I made a mistake with it. I used my big green plastic Tupperware bowl in the microwave that I had owned for 25 years, and it ended up with a hole melted in it. I learned my lesson! So, be warned, and don't repeat my mistake—make sure you use a microwave-safe bowl.

*Blue Ribbon Tip*
Times may vary according to microwave ovens. If a lower wattage microwave oven is used, the mixture may need to cook longer by about a minute or two.

# Lemon Pudding Icebox Dessert

*This dessert is so refreshing. It's also easy to make and take to a friend after they've had a baby or surgery—or just to share!*

*Makes 8 to 10 servings*

1    **(14.3-ounce) package cream-filled golden sandwich cookies\*, crushed**

6    **tablespoons salted butter, melted**

1    **(8-ounce) package cream cheese, softened**

3¼   **cups plus 2 tablespoon whole milk, divided**

¼    **cup white sugar**

3½   **cups frozen whipped topping\*, thawed, divided**

1    **(3.9-ounce) box instant lemon pudding**

1. In a medium bowl, combine crushed cookies and melted butter. Scatter into a 13x9-inch pan and chill until firm, about 1 hour.

2. In a medium bowl, beat cream cheese with hand mixer at medium speed until light and fluffy. Gradually incorporate 2 tablespoons milk and sugar, and stir in 1½ cups whipped topping until combined. Spread filling onto chilled crust.

3. In a medium bowl, whisk together pudding and remaining 3¼ cups milk until lightly thickened. Spread over cream cheese mixture. Allow to chill for 5 minutes or until thickened. Spread remaining 2 cups whipped topping over the pudding layer. Cover and refrigerate for up to 4 hours.

*\*I use Golden Oreo Cookies and Cool Whip.*

## Santa

Cookies are baking in the oven
Oh they smell so good
Always very tasty
Like you know they would.

Lights on the Christmas tree
Are shining pretty and bright,
There's magic in the air
On this special night.

Santa will enjoy the cookies and milk
That you leave on your table
He will laugh and be jolly of
That he is very able.

He will leave good boys and girls
Presents under the tree
And maybe a nice gift
For Daddy and me.

When the kids wake up that morning
And see presents under the tree
They will be so happy
And start shouting with glee.

Paper, ribbons, and bows
Are thrown across the floor
When the kids see their gifts
Their spirits soar.

# Brownies with Frosting

*My nephew Jerry Wayne has said he could smell my brownies
from a mile away. I feel sure he meant that in a good way.
He definitely seemed to like them well enough!*

*Makes about 24*

1     **cup plus 1 tablespoon salted butter**
¾     **cup unsweetened cocoa powder**
1½   **cups all-purpose flour**
1     **teaspoon baking powder**
1     **teaspoon table salt**
4     **large eggs, room temperature**
2     **cups white sugar**
1     **teaspoon vanilla extract**
**Frosting (recipe follows)**

1. Preheat oven to 350°. Grease a 13x9-inch pan.

2. In a small saucepan, melt butter over medium-low heat; remove from heat and stir in cocoa powder. Let cool completely.

3. In a small bowl, whisk together flour, baking powder, and salt.

4. In a medium bowl, whisk together eggs and sugar. Gradually incorporate the flour mixture, and whisk in vanilla and cooled chocolate mixture until fully combined.

5. Spread brownie batter into prepared pan, and bake until a wooden pick inserted in the center comes out clean, 25 to 28 minutes. Let cool completely on a wire rack. Remove the cooled brownies from the pan, spread with Frosting, and cut into individual pieces.

**FROSTING:**
6     **tablespoon salted butter, softened**
2⅔   **cups powdered sugar**
½     **cup unsweetened cocoa powder**
1     **teaspoon vanilla extract**
⅓     **cup whole milk**

1. In a medium mixing bowl, beat butter, sugar, cocoa, and vanilla with hand mixer. Gradually stir in the milk, adding just enough to get the frosting to spreading consistency. (You may not need the full ⅓ cup milk.)

# Strawberry Fudge

*This is one of my newer recipes and is based on a recipe that a family friend, Catherine Justice, shared with me. I always love swapping recipes with friends and learning to make new things.*

*Makes 1 (8x8-inch) pan*

3    **cups white chocolate chips**
½    **cup salted butter**
1    **(14-ounce) can sweetened condensed milk**
2    **(0.8-ounce) packages freeze-dried strawberries, chopped**
1    **teaspoon vanilla extract**

1. Line and grease an 8x8-inch pan with foil.

2. In a large microwave-safe bowl, microwave chocolate chips, butter, and condensed milk on medium, stirring in 30-second intervals until melted and smooth. Add strawberries and vanilla; mix well. Pour into prepared pan. Chill until set, about 4 hours. Cut into pieces and serve. Store leftover fudge in the refrigerator.

## Christmas at My House

I love getting ready for Christmas
All the decorations on my tree
It is the happiest time of year
On that I will agree.

All the pretty lights of my tree
Shine and glisten on every hook
I just want to sit
And take a long look.

The best part of Christmas
Is when my family comes here
They make me so happy
Each one I hold dear.

We gather to eat our food
That I've made for us to share
The love I have for them
Shows I care.

I watch the little ones
Open presents and shout with joy
Something for everyone
And each girl and boy.

The time goes by way too fast
And they have to leave and go home
And Dad and I
Are sitting here alone.

# Cookie Balls

*I make these at Christmas every year. They are a big favorite in my family and with my friends.
I love that they're only 3 ingredients—it makes for an easy and cost-effective dessert.*

*Makes about 30*

1   (14.3-ounce) package cream filled
     chocolate sandwich cookies*, crushed
1   (8-ounce) package cream cheese, softened
1½  pounds white chocolate chips

1. Line a large baking sheet with wax paper.

2. In a large bowl, mix together chocolate sandwich
cookies and cream cheese. Roll into 1-inch balls
and refrigerate until firm, about 1 hour.

3. In a microwave-safe bowl, melt chocolate
chips according to package directions. Dip
balls in white chocolate, letting excess chocolate
drip off, and place on wax paper. (If the
chocolate gets too hard while dipping, heat
in the microwave for a few seconds and stir.)
Let stand for 15 minutes or until set.

*I use Oreo Cookies.

# Fudge Cut-Outs

*These are really cute to make for any holiday. I use whatever cookie cutters I have that match the season.*

*Makes 1 (13x9-inch) pan*

**3**    **cups semi-sweet chocolate chips**
**1**    **(14-ounce) can sweetened condensed milk**
**⅛**    **teaspoon table salt**
**1**    **cup walnuts, chopped**
**1½**  **teaspoons vanilla extract**

1. Line and grease a 13x9-inch baking pan with foil, letting excess extend over sides of pan.

2. In a large microwave-safe bowl, microwave chocolate chips, condensed milk, and salt on medium for 1 minute. Stir well and microwave 15–30 seconds more or until chocolate melts. Stir in walnuts and vanilla, and spread into prepared pan. Refrigerate for 2 hours or until firm.

3. Lift out of pan and remove foil. Cut into desired shapes with cookie cutters or cut into pieces. Chill until ready to serve.

# RECIPE INDEX

## APPETIZERS, SNACKS & DIPS

Bacon Broccoli Cheese Ball 55
Cheese-Stuffed Jalapeños 70
Cornflake Clusters 62
Dilly Pretzels 74
Dip for Fries 54
Ham Rolls 65
Pimento Cheese Spread 44
Pineapple Cheese Ball 51
Sausage Balls 73
Sausage Pinwheels 76
Southwestern Dip 47
Strawberry Dip 48
Taco Dip 52
Veggie Bars 69
White Chocolate Peanut Butter Crackers 66
Weenies in BBQ Sauce 77

## BREAD

Buttermilk Biscuits 187
Cheesy-Garlic Biscuits 179
Hush Puppies 175
Mexican Cornbread 183
Pineapple Zucchini Bread 176
Red Chili Biscuits 184
Rolls 180
Zucchini Cornbread 172

## CANNING

Blackberry Jam 21
Bread-and-Butter Pickles 29
Canned Peaches 37
Canned Tomatoes 33
Chow Chow 18
Corn Relish 38
Grape Jelly 39
Jalapeño Salsa 34
Peach-Raspberry Jam 22
Pickled Banana Peppers 30
Pickled Beets 26
Pumpkin Butter 188
Slow Cooker Apple Butter 188
Strawberry Jam 25

## DESSERTS & SWEETS

Banana Pudding Poke Cake 198
Brownies with Frosting 248
Candy Bar Fudge 236
Carrot Cake 197
Chocolate Chip Cookies 224
Coconut Cake 205
Cookie Balls 252
Creamsicle Fudge 243
Dump Cake 209
Frozen Strawberry Pie 228
Fudge Cut-Outs 253
Ginger Ale Pound Cake 194
Hornet's Nest Cake 213
Jam Cake with Caramel Glaze 202
Lemon Pudding Icebox Dessert 247
Molasses Cake 214
No-Bake Butterscotch Cookies 231
No-Bake Peanut Butter Cookies 230
Nutty Buddy Pie 227
Oatmeal Cake 206
Oatmeal Cookies 220
Peach Hand Pies 223
Peanut Brittle 244
Peanut Butter Fudge 239
Piña Colada Fudge 240
Pumpkin Sheet Cake with Cream Cheese Icing 210
Strawberry Fudge 251
Sugarless Spice Cake 201

## MAIN DISHES

BBQ Shredded Chicken Sandwiches 106
Buffalo Chicken Pizza 109
Cabbage Roll Casserole 141
Creamy Cheesy Spaghetti 110
Enchilada Casserole 138
Fried Catfish 114
Homestyle Meat Loaf 118
Lasagna 117
Pineapple Baked Ham 121
Pot Roast 122
Salmon Cakes 125
Slow Cooker Cabbage Rolls 113
Sourdough Steak 126
Spaghetti & Meatballs 129
Super Chicken Casserole 142

## SOUPS, SALADS, & SIDES

Beef Stew 85
Broccoli Casserole 134
Broccoli Cheese Soup 82
Chicken Salad 98
Chili 89
Coleslaw 167
Cornbread Dressing 152
Cornbread Salad 90
Corn Casserole 146
Cowboy Beans 156
Deviled Eggs 166
Garlic Mashed Potatoes 159
Golden Parmesan Potatoes 163
Granny Smith Apple Salad 93
Hashbrown Potato Casserole 145
Loaded Red Potato Casserole 137
Mac & Cheese 164
Orange Fruit Salad 86
Oven-Fried Green Tomatoes 155
Parmesan Baked Squash 160
Pasta Salad 99
Potato Soup 94
Taco Soup 97

## EVERYTHING ELSE

Apple Sauce Ornaments 235
Caramel Glaze 202
Cream Cheese Frosting 210
Frosting 248
Holiday Spice Potpourri 235
Peanut Butter Balls 219
Peanut Butter Dog Treats 219
Sausage Gravy 188
Sourdough Starter 126

## A Final Note of Thanks

THANK YOU TO ALL MY FRIENDS who have helped me and encouraged me through the years. I'm eternally grateful to have such a wonderful community supporting me. I'm thankful for all my family has done to make this book happen. Frank has helped tirelessly in ways that I can't fully encompass in a few short words. He's a great husband and an even better man, who has supported me so much on this journey. I'm lucky to have him by my side through this life. My children mean so much to me. Frank Jr. encouraged me to enter my first fair. Without him, I would never have gotten my first blue ribbon all those years ago. Elizabeth is endless in her support and always my biggest advocate. Cathy has been the linchpin for the whole operation. Without her, it would have fallen apart long ago. She's driven me to interviews, reviewed contracts, helped with my social media, and so much more.

Also, I want to give a special thanks to my friends at Hoffman Media and 83 Press who helped publish my cookbook. Anna, my editor, has helped me through every step of the process to make sure that my recipes and memories work together to share my story in these pages. Jennifer turned all my handwritten notes and family photos into my dream cookbook full of her beautiful designs. Kristi helped us with social media and gave us countless video tips. Donna, Vanessa, Kathleen, Jim, and Kyle came to visit me in Virginia and helped photograph me in my home and at the fair. You all made my food and recipes really shine. There are countless others who have worked on this project over the last few months, and I'm forever grateful for the time and energy you have dedicated to me, my family, and this book.

Additionally, I want to extend my gratitude to all the people who work so hard to put on county fairs every year. Your tireless work helps keep a time-honored tradition alive. To those at the Virginia-Kentucky District Fair, the Russell County Fair, and the Washington County Fair, you have put on wonderful fairs year after year. It's an honor to compete.

Finally, thank you to all the people in the news and on social media who asked the question, "Who is Linda Skeens?" Thank you for finding me and giving me an opportunity to answer that question. A special thanks goes to my new friend, Mason Moussette, who searched for me and gave me my first chance to tell my story. I'm a simple cook with simple recipes (and a competitive nature), and because of you all, I got to realize my dream of writing a cookbook.

I hope my story encourages you to follow your own dreams. You never know where they might lead. God bless you, all.

*Linda Skeens*